tantra for gay men

tantra
for gay men

BRUCE ANDERSON

alyson books
los angeles | new york

MANUFACTURED IN THE UNITED STATES OF AMERICA.

THIS TRADE PAPERBACK ORIGINAL IS PUBLISHED BY ALYSON PUBLICATIONS,
P.O. BOX 4371, LOS ANGELES, CALIFORNIA 90078-4371.
DISTRIBUTION IN THE UNITED KINGDOM BY
TURNAROUND PUBLISHER SERVICES LTD.,
UNIT 3, OLYMPIA TRADING ESTATE, COBURG ROAD, WOOD GREEN,
LONDON N22 6TZ ENGLAND.

FIRST EDITION: NOVEMBER 2002

02 03 04 05 06 a 10 9 8 7 6 5 4 3 2 1

ISBN 1-55583-749-2

COVER DESIGN BY MATT SAMS.
INTERIOR PHOTOGRAPHS BY BRUCE ANDERSON.

Contents

Acknowledgments

Many people have profoundly influenced the creation of this book. My teachers, Swami Anadanakapila and Umeshanand, have deepened my understanding of myself and the universe around me. They have always been just an E-mail or phone call away, guiding me with open hearts, inspiring me, and challenging me, and I owe them great thanks.

Without my skilled editor, Scott Brassart, who identified a need in the gay community for this material and sought me out to fill that need, this book would not exist. I am indebted to him for his vision, support, and damn good editing. I also wish to thank my dear friend Stephen Schlanser, who graciously provided me with the opportunity to come to Mexico and stay at his second home, where I composed the body of the book. Above all, this book would never have been written if not for the loving support, beauty, and care that my life partner, Kenneth Symington, has provided me for over 20 years. I have much more to thank him for than this modest section could possibly contain.

Finally, I would like to thank Nature herself. She has played a significant role in both my life and the development of this book, which was conceived high in the Canadian Rockies, developed on the peaceful shores of Mexico's Banderas Bay, and finished in beautiful Tamil Nadu, South India.

x

Om Shiva,
Bruce Anderson
Pondicherry, Tamil Nadu, India

Introduction
The River

 I stopped my hike and quietly looked around. Through the canopy of tall Douglas fir and western spruce, the sun filtered down into the forest, turning the aspen leaves white and the maple leaves chartreuse, before coming to rest on the plants of the forest floor: ferns, trillium, and the small berries that feed the creatures of the woods.

I walked onward and came to a small brook bouncing over rocks, winding through fallen wood, and pooling to create mirrors of the forest ceiling and the sky. A path alongside and through the streambed beckoned me, and I followed its gentle downhill slope, carefully picking stepping-stones as I took great care to leave no footprint, no trace; I was a welcome guest respectful of the beauty the forest provided. Maidenhair ferns nodded gently as

I walked by; birds at the tops of the trees called to each other. Were they announcing my arrival? Who would want to know?

The farther I hiked, the faster and surer I felt about my journey along this little creek. Rivulets flowed from the banks, and the stream swelled as cool spring water bubbled into it. At one point, orange stones announced a mineral pool pouring into the creek, creating a slight sulfur smell and warming the water ever so gently.

2

I continue down, the streambed now twice as wide. The stones are larger, smoother, but farther apart. I have to jump now to stay dry.

I hear rapids around the next bend and move from the stepping-stones to the bank. There is more sunlight now, as the widening water has created a break in the forest canopy. Swaths of sunlight pour down into the rushing crystal-clear water, transforming the stones into gems. Leaves catch the light, and along their edges reflect it back to other leaves, branches, tree trunks, and into my eyes. I stand spellbound in the midst of beauty.

I round the bend, and the rapids come into view. A series of stones causes the water to churn and froth, making it appear dangerous, white with chaos and vitality, saturated with energy, ecstatic and destructive. The roaring fills my ears, drowning the birdcalls and the sound of the wind. I make my way carefully and slowly along the bank. But before I see the end of the rapids, I find a brief shaded resting-place.

I sit with my knees drawn up, but my back soon complains. So I lie down and feel my back, arms, head, and neck melt into the soft bank. The verdant smells of the very alive forest cover me like mist. I am immobile, unable to move, and I sink farther into the soil.

While my body rests on the shore, my mind is called to continue traveling. *I rise from my body and fly at lightning speed, rising higher, ever higher, above the treetops and toward the sun. With every breath I feel my lightness, my self at its most beautiful and inspired. I fly into a cloud bank and am startled by what I see.*

Behind the veil of clouds lies a city—a place of minarets, domed buildings, temples, and altars of gold shining radiantly white. The city is peopled with gods and demigods. I am guided, it feels, to a building with a temple inside. The doorway is small, but the building is not. It is cavernous. I step forward to a simple altar. Above me is an opening; a circle of light in the dome illuminates the altar and the room it's in. I close my eyes and at this altar am gifted with the vision of creation—worlds being born; the ecstasy of life emerging, bursting forth, unfolding in time. I hold my breath in awe as worlds dissolve. I feel the fear of life ebbing. I see simultaneous death in birth—of planets, galaxies, knowledge, healing, and hurt. The intensity of the vision overwhelms me, and I am in tears. The beauty is amazing and otherworldly.

4

It is divinity.

It is the all-powerful Generator, Operator, and Dissolver that God is.

I move to another room, where I look through a window covered with a grille and see only primary colors, as if from a prism, hovering around every edge, every surface. As I observe creation, I feel myself dissolve and transcend my meager human frame. I am again borne aloft, this time by the soaring music that lines the edges of clouds in the city of God.

The sun streams hotly on my face. Sweating, I become aware of my surroundings. I open my eyes and see the same prismatic primary colors along the edges of the huckleberry bushes and the cedar bark. The stones in the stream have grown into boulders, the water into a roar of strength.

I was so moved that I could not move. I remained motionless, at one with the soil, the forest, the sun, unable to feel my hands or arms or legs, indivisible with creation. I felt at peace and indelibly changed.

part one

The History,
Philosophy,
and Relevance
of Tantra
for Gay Men

Chapter One
What is Tantra?

While Tantra is one of the most powerful approaches to spiritual development, it is also among the most misunderstood—not only here in the West, but at its home in India. Thus, my goal in writing this book is first to provide a basic understanding of Tantra and then lay out a series of exercises designed to help you incorporate Tantric ritual into your life. The information I present in this volume comes from many years of study in the Americas and India and reflects what I have learned on my quest for spiritual enlightenment and ecstatic bliss. I invite you to approach this material with an active mind, testing and evaluating to see what works for you. Hopefully, you will be pleased with the results and will seek further tutelage in the mysteries of Tantra.

The term *Tantra* is derived from two Sanskrit words, *tan* and *tra*. *Tan* means "tools," and *tra* means "expansion." Thus, at its core Tantra means "tools for

expansion." The Sanskrit stem *tan* survives in English in words like tangible, meaning touchable. Not surprisingly, Tantric tools for expansion are body-based, experiential, and full of touch—tangible.

Readers of this book may be more familiar with the word *mantra* that describes the repetition of a sacred sound or sounds, like *om*. The word mantra is derived from *manas,* Sanskrit for "mind," and *tra,* meaning "expansion." Thus, by practicing mantra, you expand your mind. Mantra is a specific technique used in Tantra and other yogic practices.

10

मानस त्र

It's nearly impossible to pinpoint the origins of Tantra because it dates back to a time before alphabets were in use and because the word itself comes from a language that was a precursor to Sanskrit. We do, however, have some idea and understanding of the environment in which Tantra originated.

The story begins 6,000 years ago in a place known today as the Indus Valley. The people who  lived there had a deep and personal relationship with their environment. The earth was likened to a cornucopia providing food, water, pleasure, delight, and ecstasy. Nature was responsible for birth and generating life, sustaining and preserving life, and also for ending life.

From this understanding grew the religion of

Shaivism. Shaivism centers on worship of the Hindu god Shiva, who is one aspect of the Divine. (As Christians developed a strict religion based on the teachings of Christ, Lutherans on the teachings of Luther, and Buddhists on the teachings of Buddha, Shaivites created their religion through direct revelation with the god Shiva.) Shaivism is a mystical religion that promotes the joy of living. Shaivites view the natural world as representing the divine work of the gods. Their approach is ecstatic, orgiastic, and ritualistic. Like all ancient religions, Shaivism was transmitted orally and through hands-on initiation. Shaivism still exists, though it is now more temple-based than nature-based.

Language at the time of early Shaivism was much different than language today. Six thousand years ago, people in that part of the world communicated by means of an almost completely extinct language group known as *agglutinating.* Agglutinating languages are comprised of small fragments woven together to create word sentences. In agglutinating languages everything is of equal merit and value—birth, sustenance, and death. Thus, God is immediate and tangible.

Later languages, such as Sanskrit and its great-grandchild, English, are more structured and are described by linguists as causal. Causal languages are based on hierarchies. All of the parts are not equal. In causal languages some words carry greater importance than others do. For instance, in English, importance is conveyed by word order. In the sentence "Dog bites man," the dog is taking the action, the man receiving. We know this based on word order. Conversely, the reordered sentence "Man bites dog" conveys a much different meaning.

This distinction is important in understanding the origins of Tantra because agglutinating languages produce inclusive systems (woven together like a basket), whereas causal languages create exclusive systems (structured in levels like a ladder). Shaivism, born at a time of agglutinating languages, understands the importance of all forms of life. Later religions such as Hinduism are more hierarchical. In fact, the ancient and strict Hindu caste system still exists today. Even the great political leader Mahatma Gandhi was unable to break the caste system.

Consequently, our understanding of traditional and original Tantra requires us to be flexible in our thinking—a challenge because our English language structure predisposes us to hierarchical rather than inclusive thinking.

Unfortunately, there are no writings about Tantra that predate Sanskrit. Thus, the extant Tantras (writings that describe Tantra) are causal language translations, many of which were sustained and preserved (and interpreted) by Buddhists, Hindus, Kashmiris, and Jains. Many other Tantric writings were destroyed during the Islamic invasion and later during the European colonization of India. Thus, our understanding of Tantra in its original form is limited.

There is, however, much that we do know. For instance, Tantra is closely linked to Shaivism. In fact, the Tantras are the rites and rituals of the Shaiva religion. Shaivism has eight other disciplines: the traditions, the ancient chronicles, cosmology, yoga, linguistics, astronomy, medicine, and mathematics.

One Tantric ritual is regular penis worship. More specifically, worshiping the god Shiva's penis, known in Sanskrit as *lingam*.

This worship of Shiva's erection continues today not only in Shaivism but also in Hindu rituals. This is primarily true of fertility rituals, such as when a phallic stone inserted into a replica of a *yoni* (Sanskrit for vagina) is anointed as part of *puja* (worship service), sometimes with ejaculate-like

white yogurt. The yoni is seen as a source of life equal to the lingam. In Tantra, both lingam and yoni exist in everyone; they are neither gender-bound nor genitalia-specific.

In Shaivism, the god Shiva is the highest male divine principle. He is continuously making love with his consort and thereby creating all of the known and unknown universe. The entire universe is believed to have emanated from Shiva's penis. Thus, both men and women worship his erection.

From this stems the Shaivistic philosophy that our world is continual sensual delight. A household altar in a Shaivite's home includes a lingam, and daily worship services center around veneration of the divine sacred phallus.

16

It is interesting to note that in Shaivism there exists no taboo or restriction as to sexual or erotic expression. All sexuality is celebrated as a facet of the Divine and of the natural order of the universe. This not only gives permission for same-sex expressions of love but also honors and sanctifies the love between two men as holy and godlike.

In fact, Shiva had a son, Skanda, who in today's society would likely be regarded as a gay man. Skanda, whose name literally translates to "jet of sperm," sprang to life as some of

Shiva's sperm dripped down to earth and was swallowed by fire. Skanda's only spouse was his army, and he was hostile to the idea of marriage. There is historical evidence that homosexuals in ancient India worshiped Skanda. And as the god of beauty and perpetual youth, he could easily serve as the patron saint for many gay men today.

It is important to note that although its rituals are closely linked with Shaivism, Tantra itself is not a religion. You can practice Tantric rituals as a Christian, Jew, Muslim, Buddhist, pagan, or anything else. Tantra is simply an approach to living designed to bring its practitioners closer to the Divine. For example, gyms are full of men of many faiths, worshiping communally at the altar of the body. They are methodically transforming themselves into objects of greater beauty. Although some gym bunnies may be superficial, merely wanting to look good, it is possible for them to incorporate Tantra into their daily routines, thereby turning their workouts into a deepening spiritual experience.

MY JOURNEY FROM
EVANGELICAL CHRISTIANITY TO TANTRA

I grew up in an Evangelical Christian family. I was taught that conforming to the strict teachings of our church would lead to eternal life in heaven, and that to not conform would lead to a horrible, unending death. My family and religion did a magnificent job of scaring me witless, gutless, and guileless, driving a wedge between my head and my heart. Consequently, I lived a bloodless, soulless, and very depressed life.

Of course, not everything about my childhood was bad. My father made certain I had regular access to the outdoors, even though we lived in a city. We had a summerhouse in a national forest, and in my adolescence I spent many weekends hiking and observing nature. Spending so much time in nature presented me with an understanding of the cycles of life, and of the beautiful, intricate, and delicate balance between all living creatures. Perhaps more importantly, I learned that nature is never depressed. Plants and trees always grow to their greatest potential given soil quality, light, and water. Always. They never give up; they simply keep striving. This knowledge helped me through many difficult periods.

While my father gave me the outdoors, my mother gave me music. I began piano lessons at age 6, and by 10 I was performing in monthly recitals. Music provided me with solace and a personal, private place to express myself emotionally. I threw myself into it, practicing piano and the violin for up to six hours a day. I performed with an orchestra at 14 and won composition awards starting at 15.

My mother also gave me a thirst for spirituality. As a very religious family, we were seemingly always in church. Sometimes when singing hymns, an uplifting feeling would come over me, and I would feel deeply connected to everything—a similar feeling to when I was out in nature or performing.

Soon, however, I grew to understand that I was gay. I was old enough to understand that this made me different, and that in the eyes of my family and my religion my longings were sinful. Even worse, there was no one with whom I could share my feelings. I felt achingly alone. I impulsively quit the piano at age 17 after losing in a competition. And two years later, when a hand injury forced me to quit the violin as well, I was secretly pleased. I understand now that I was depressed and my heart was no longer in it.

At 22, I found myself living in Philadelphia, the City of Brotherly Love. Unfortunately, I felt no such love. One day, loneliness and the pressure of beginning an academic career at an Ivy League school were too much to bear. While grocery shopping in Center City, I started crying for no apparent reason—in the canned soup aisle, of all places.

I decided I needed to reach out. I tried talk therapy, first with an incompetent Freudian analyst, later with a social worker who helped me find the courage and hope to come out as a gay man and live a life true to my inner self.

20

I later found out there was a spiritual practice that included sexual expression, and I immediately wanted to learn as much as possible about it. Looking back, I realize I was driven by a desire to understand the relationship between God and sex. Happily, through a succession of teachers starting with Joseph Kramer, who led me to Bodhi Avinasha, who led me to Sunyata Saraswati, who led me to Swami Anandakapila Saraswati, I have begun to understand the beautiful, deeply moving spiritual technology of Tantra. I have learned how to unify my self and my spirit through music, nature, and sex. Through new experiences, my awareness has expanded, my relationships have deepened, and my capacity for feeling and empathy has increased.

I have experienced the bliss of Tantric experience.

Tantra and Being Gay

All of the teachings of Tantra are applicable to gay men. In fact, it is my belief that Tantra is the spiritual path most appropriate for gay men in the 21st century. This is because the Tantric experience in many ways parallels the gay experience, thereby making Tantra conceptually accessible to gay men, despite its inclusive rather than hierarchical nature. I believe gay men are more easily able to accept an inclusive system that does not conform to the social norm because gay men, by their very nature, are outsiders with a different perspective on life and how to live it. Our outsider status gives us a great opportunity for unique insight.

Not surprisingly, the god Shiva is often viewed as the enemy of human convention. Just as male/male sexual practices run against cultural norms, so do many Tantric practices—partaking of forbidden foods and drink, allowing women and people from multiple castes to worship together, etc.

There are numerous other parallels between Tantra and contemporary gay culture. For instance, traditional Tantra and contemporary gay culture both celebrate ecstatically and orgiastically. From circuit parties to AIDS rides to fisting scenes, gay culture is constantly pushing both physical and spiritual limits. Similarly, Tantric practice expands consciousness and provides physical bliss through ritual and sexual worship. Both also share a diversity of expression and experience: Just as Tantra venerates many aspects of the Divine, represented as gods and goddesses, gay men worship at multiple altars—bears and cubs, drag and drugs, leather and lace.

Furthermore, both Tantra and gay culture can be experienced solo, as a pair, or in groups. In the Neo-Tantrist heterosexual world (a popular American sexual movement following the Bhagwan Sri Rajneesh's arrival in North America), there is a myth that people need a partner to expand their consciousness through Tantra. However, this is contradicted by a truth of traditional Tantra: Every experience you have is *your* experience. It is a solo experience and at the same time a connecting experience to all of life as experienced in *your* body. Sometimes, it's easier to expand your consciousness by yourself, since the dimension of another man can hold you back. This is not to say that great experiences can't be had with a partner or in groups.

An aspect of Tantra that has received significant popular attention (in part because of the Bhagwan Shree Rajneesh) is its erotic/sexual dimension. In fact, when I tell people I teach Tantra, they usually raise their eyebrows and smile nervously. However, it is important to realize that although the erotic dimension is central to aspects of Tantra, it is actually only a small portion of Tantric ritual.

That said, the most obvious parallel between Tantra and contemporary gay culture is celebration and worship of the penis. Central to Tantra and

many Hindu practices is the daily worship of Shiva's erection, known as Shiva lingam. In gay culture, some men are so erection-focused that they transform their bodies into tight packages that resemble large, throbbing, veiny penises.

The rituals known as Tantra are actions of power. Tantra is deeply mystical, and its practice leads to a personal experience of the Divine. Tantra offers a map for spiritual development. With Tantra, we can grow safely and securely while exploring and expanding our consciousness, spirituality, and sexuality. The remainder of this book is designed to give a better understanding of what Tantra is and to provide exercises and rituals that will allow you to incorporate Tantric practice into your daily life.

24

Chapter Two
The goal of Tantra

"WHAT IS HERE IS ELSEWHERE;
WHAT IS NOT HERE IS NOWHERE."
—VISVASHARATANTRA

"AS ABOVE, SO BELOW."
—WESTERN MYSTICAL MAXIM

All technique has a goal or an intended result, and Tantra is no exception, although one of the goals of Tantra—to have no goal—may seem to contradict this statement. This will be explained momentarily. Other goals of Tantra are to attain spiritual bliss, and to expand our understanding of our exoteric nature as well as our esoteric anatomy.

Two building blocks of traditional Tantra are mantra and yantra. Mantra is the practice of repeating sacred sounds. These sounds emit a vibration that changes us and modifies our thinking, leading to a new emotional state—important because our emotions lead us to the threshold of Divinity.

Yantra is the geometric representation of the sacred sounds of mantra. (Since sound is a vibration, it has a shape, which can be recorded and represented geometrically.) Yantras are used for meditation, to focus the mind and heart, as a charm, or to invoke a deity.

26

Mantra and yantra are the two links between the human and the divine worlds. They are used in traditional Tantra as techniques to approach the Divine. For example, you would chant a very specific mantra to invite a deity to be present, and you would also draw a yantra to make your energies congruent with your intentions.

For our purposes, we will use the mantra *om*. Tantra and other yogic disciplines consider *om* the seed sound of creation. It usually precedes and concludes a full mantra. *Om* is easy to remember, and chanting it either alone or with a partner brings you into a sacred vibration.

At the beginners' level of Tantric practice, we consider as *sacred* an emotional and spiritual space that is distinctly different from ordinary space. A good analogy is how Roman Catholics genuflect and walk in a specific way to honor their beliefs while in a Roman Catholic Church. (Before the Vatican II reforms, these practices were even more pronounced.)

In more advanced Tantric practice, however, Tantra is present in everyday life, thereby eliminating the sacred versus mundane split. Incorporation of the sacred into all aspects of life is the ultimate goal of Tantra. Thus, the goal of Tantra is to have no goal—because you are already operating from a position of divinity.

There is a branch of Tantra where specific charms and rituals are utilized to obtain specific, tangible results. Some of these—power, wealth, luck—would not always be considered "spiritual." However, that branch of Tantra is not the focus of this book. Our discussion focuses only on Tantra as a direct path to individual enlightenment and bliss.

As we develop to a place of greater daily spiritual expression, there are numerous human bonds we must overcome. The Kularnavatantra—the surviving scriptures of a branch of Tantra known as Kaula—lists these succinctly. Surprisingly, they sound like a list of psychotherapy accomplishments. According to this text, the serious student will need to overcome pity, ignorance, shame, family, custom, and caste. Although in the West we do not live in the traditional Hindu caste system, we do have castes based on race, ethnicity, sexual orientation, wealth, education, and many other factors. Anyone who has tried to move from blue-collar to white-collar work can attest to this. Such movement requires the development of new verbal and nonverbal communication skills, a different style of dress, and possibly even the adoption of different core values.

28

It should be noted that there are many different aspects of the Divine. In Hindu thought, gods and goddesses represent these different aspects. The three main aspects of the Divine—Generation (creation), Operation (preserving and sustaining), and Dissolution (returning to the source)—are all known as *leela,* best defined as "divine play." This is an important concept in Tantra, since all of the natural world is sacred. As humans, we are here to align ourselves with this sacredness by making all of our life a form of leela.

As the Divine is recognized to have many forms, we may worship multiple aspects of God: Shiva; his consort, Shakti; his son, Skanda; the man-elephant god, Ganesha; the bloodthirsty goddess, Kali; and many others. This is similar to Roman Catholics worshiping Mary, mother of Jesus, along with the Holy Trinity of God, Jesus, and the Holy Spirit. Even in ostensibly monotheistic Christianity, the concept of God is too big to personify in one anthropomorphic figure.

That said, a warning is in order: Invoking the gods can be a dangerous practice. In 1993 I was with a group of Neo-Tantrists. We began a ritual that lasted for several days by invoking and inviting the goddess Kali. The goddess revealed herself, and the whole group fell into dissolution, with many of the men so frightened they ran as fast as possible away from the ritual. Hours later, we bade Kali farewell and the group resumed. Our invocation, though deeply spiritual, was ill placed, naive, and shortsighted. We were the sorcerer's apprentices, the ones who had just enough knowledge to be dangerous. Our invocation of Kali was indeed leela, but the risk of severe suffering was in our human dimension. With better preparation and care, we could have prevented the destructive aspect of Kali wielding her sword in our group. Thus, it is imperative to educate oneself before launching into the use of Tantric rituals. Otherwise, your mantras and yantras may not achieve the intended result.

30

Chapter Three
how Tantra works

In Tantra, nature is the bridge between dense matter, or *tamas* (that which veils), and light, or *sattva* (that which reveals). The process of moving from tamas to sattva is accomplished by *rajas* (taking action). By observing a simple plant, we can witness this process: The plant rises from its seed, and through the action of growing and reaching for light it attains its fullest possible realization.

When this line of thought is applied to human experience, we view our spirit as our true nature, our sattva, initially hidden within the shell of the body, or that which veils us: tamas. We take action, rajas, to uncover our inner light. The actions taken could be reading, observing, worshiping, chanting, or anything else that supports our higher purpose.

Through observation, the ancient sages arrived at the very modern concept of learning. For me, learning means that when confronted with a situation similar to one I've previously experienced, I rely on the memory of that previous experience when deciding what new action to take in the present to achieve the most desired/beneficial outcome. (This is the opposite of how most 12-step recovery programs define insanity: taking the same action over and over, but expecting different results.) Given that every moment is fresh and new, repeating old actions can never yield the most beneficial result.

The ancient sages also found through observation that the process of learning, as defined above, illustrates the spiritual development of each of us. In Tantric practice, we take action, rajas, to illuminate our inherent spirit, our sattva. These actions include initiation, education, worship, and daily practice.

INITIATION

To initiate means literally to begin. In Tantra, this beginning may be one of several formal ceremonies with a teacher—instruction in mantra, receiving a sacred name, or the teacher placing his

hands on the student and transmitting a spiritual quickening.

Initiation is not unique to Tantra. Other spiritual practices also have forms of initiation. For instance, in Roman Catholicism there is baptism, confirmation, and the power of apostolic succession (the power to confer the Eucharist—to transubstantiate wine and wafers into the blood and body of Jesus).

I have been blessed with several Tantra initiations, including an initiation to teach Tantra and to initiate my students into a particular breath technique called Nagapranayama. The details of the initiation rituals I have experienced are too intimate to me to share in writing. It is my hope that you will eventually experience your own Tantra initiation and then understand my reticence about discussing this topic.

EDUCATION

In today's society, the primary motivation for learning is to avoid pain. We are taught to behave in a certain way, and that if we don't we'll be punished. At a very basic level, this experience is contrary to that of Tantra: gaining knowledge that leads to ever-expanding spiritual understanding and development. In fact, our learning systems today—especially our religious educational systems—serve primarily to indoctrinate rather than educate.

The Latin root of both *education* and *indoctrination* is *ducere,* meaning "to lead." The prefix *e* in education means "out of." Thus, education is the process of leading one out of darkness and into light, of providing greater choices and an enlarged worldview. A similar concept in Sanskrit is *jnana,* defined as "knowledge that liberates."

Conversely, the prefix *in* in indoctrination means "into." Thus, indoctrination is the process of leading one into knowledge that confines and restricts. Indoctrination systems are typically ascetic, rule-bound, and limiting. Followers of such systems often seem to wander soullessly through the world, following some great spiritual cookbook while dead to the joys of life.

Tantra offers a path of spiritual *education* that allows us to fully delve into the human endeavor with all its contradictions, paradoxes, messiness, chaos, dissolution, and creation. In other words, Tantra offers jnana. The beginning point is now, the place is here, and the first process is observation and examination, presence and awareness.

We can also view jnana as the psychological concept of individuation. Individuation is a psychological term that describes the process of becoming your true self. For many, coming out as a gay man is a defining step in their individuation. It is my belief that in the process of individuation we gay men have a great advantage over our straight counterparts. Because we live outside the norm, we observe and examine life from an extra-cultural perspective; consequently, we may see more nuances as well as see differently than our nongay family members, friends, and associates. Through our own individuation as gay men, we become free from the standard societal bonds and are able to actively seek out who we authentically are.

Of course, not all men who love men are enlightened beings whose every action is a blessing to humanity, the plant kingdom, the minerals, and the Pleiades. Many gay men just substitute gay norms for the culturally dominant heterosexual ones and lead a life that confines and restricts them. There is nothing about being gay that guarantees jnana. It's simply that through our own process of self-awareness and self-acceptance we may have more choices about how we want to relate to others and view the world.

Teachers and Students

The role of the teacher in Tantra is very important. Reading about Tantra and spiritual development is useful and enlightening, but it is a little like reading about wine. You can learn the basics: how to purchase, store, and serve wine; that a proper wine complements and celebrates a meal; that champagne is not appropriate with beef Wellington, nor orange muscat with gazpacho. But this knowledge will not make you a wine master or even a connoisseur. For that you must first drink wine (akin to initiation), tasting it and feeling its effects. After that, you could eventually become a wine master through trial and error, but not without wasting vats of good wine, delaying your own enjoyment, and possibly leading others astray along the way. Whereas working with an experienced wine master, a *teacher,* would greatly expedite your education (akin to jnana).

There are many teachers of Tantra, just as there are many teachers of piano. And the most gifted teachers generally produce accomplished students. With piano, the best teachers are often artists in great demand. The analogy here is that the best teacher will help his student progress the furthest.

36

Where this analogy fails, though, is that the attainment of high degrees of spiritual development is available to anyone who dedicates himself, whereas becoming a concert pianist generally requires an initial talent that is greatly ahead of the pack. Furthermore, one may dedicate himself to a spiritual practice at any point in his life, while the onset of the path of a concert pianist usually occurs in childhood.

Let's take the piano-teacher analogy one step further. Most of the teachers of the great concert artists received direct instruction from prior great teachers. These are men and women who worked on and figured out how to execute increasingly more difficult technical and musical problems. Once they did, they were able to pass this knowledge on to the next generation, which could then augment this body of knowledge and pass that on, creating ever more competent, reliable musicians who, let's hope, increase the beauty in our world.

In my own studies, the work of Liszt had always been a remote, unfathomable mystery to me. That is, until I began working with a very gifted teacher who traced his lineage of teachers directly back to Liszt. This instructor enabled me to comprehend not only the technical aspects of performing

Liszt's compositions, but to understand the unique beauty of the composer's work.

In Tantra, there are several types of teachers—most notably swamis and gurus. Unless you hail from India, understanding Hindu and Tantra systems of teaching and learning can be confusing. Thus, a bit of explanatory historical background is in order.

38

In the 8th century ACE (After the Common Epoch), a great master and teacher, Shankara-charya, created 10 *Dasnami*, best defined as "orders" or "schools," that still exist today. Each of these Dasnami has different traditions regarding the passing down of knowledge. (It may be helpful to think of Dasnami as being similar to the various orders of the Catholic Church: Jesuits, Franciscans, Dominicans, etc.)

That said, the hierarchical structure of each of the orders is basically the same. The body of the teacher is an instrument of the highest Divine. The teacher has perfected his search for divinity. When a teacher commits to a student, he stays committed to the student while the student practices to obtain spiritual powers, or *siddhi*, such as those mentioned earlier in the brief discussion of the Kularnavatantra. Siddhis include mastering the arts of becoming small, great, light, heavy, attaining what one wills, freedom from family, freedom from society, and freedom from desires.

It is interesting to note that the Hindu hierarchical system is very similar to what we are used to in the religious institutions in the West and rather distant from the origins of Tantra. This is because, as discussed earlier, religious systems traditionally grow in ways that parallel the linguistic structure of their era. Language at the birth of Tantra was agglutinating but later evolved to causal. Religious thought has changed in a similar fashion. Even so, we can look back to a time when duality was dissolved into the eternal bliss of oneness

SWAMIS

The title *swami,* meaning "one's own master," is conferred on someone by another swami. Indian swamis frequently wear orange-colored clothes. Not all swamis are inducted into one of the 10 Dasnami. Becoming a swami is similar to the formal induction, training, and ordination of a Roman Catholic monk. A swami initiated in a particular Dasnami will have a notarized certificate and robes given to him or her upon initiation.

To become a swami is to take vows that will alter the course of your life. These vows are called *sannyas,* or renunciation. Frequently, conventional life is eschewed in order to dedicate one's attention solely to the Divine. While swamis may choose to also teach, gurus cannot choose to live as a swami unless they receive the honor of becoming a swami through initiation by another swami.

40

GURUS

The word *guru* means "one who removes darkness." While there is only one true guru—the Supreme Guru—human gurus reflect this quality in their lives. These qualities are the multifaceted expressions of enlightened bliss. There are several types of gurus. For our purposes, we will focus on two: sat gurus and upa gurus. Sat gurus are highly developed and quite rare. They can create miracles such as spontaneous healing. Historical examples are Ramakrishna, Neem Karoli Baba, and Babaji. Living sat gurus are few and far between. Ammachi is considered a sat guru, and, to his followers, Sai Baba is thought to be a sat guru.

In contrast to sat gurus, who are living saints, are upa (lesser) gurus. Upa gurus, commonly known as householder gurus, are common folk who have received advanced teachings and lead a life of spiritual pursuit as they fulfill their mundane social duties of work, family, and charity. Many upa gurus are connected to a particular sat guru through *ashrams,* or schools, established by that sat guru. My training traces back through kriya yoga to Babaji, who was born Nagaraj in 703 ACE.

In the 20th century, there has been an opening of many previously closed doors, which has made yoga and Tantra truths more accessible. One of the leaders of the Saraswati order, Satyananda, reformed his order and published many of its teachings, thus giving a great boost to both Tantra and upa gurus.

Satyananda also made it possible for householders to become Sannyasins without living a life of outer renunciation. This outer behavior of renunciation can be an artificial structure imposed on people. In Tantra, we understand renunciation with the maxim: to be in the world but not of it. We also believe it is better to learn from an upa guru than to wait for a great saint to save you. This is because we use everyday experiences as material for our spiritual growth.

Tantra has a long history of upa gurus, and in some teachings the way of the householder is seen as the supreme path. The reasoning: It is easier to isolate yourself from the world and lead a spiritual life—often supported by the donations of others—than to retain your spiritual focus while participating in everyday life.

CHELAS

42

The term *chela* means "disciple." In Tantra, the teacher, the swami or guru, is responsible to the

chela, or student. There is a long tradition of a very formal relationship between teacher and disciple. (This relationship is often distorted in the West and is sometimes abused by individuals operating at less than full integrity.) Frequently, a traditional guru-chela relationship means the guru has initiated the chela with a name that reflects the divine qualities the teacher sees in the student. My initiated name is Somananda. *Soma* is part of the esoteric anatomy, located in the head. Once initiated with a name, the disciple pledges to adhere to the responsibilities that name bears.

Earlier I mentioned that the Kularnavatantra discusses the necessity to free us from the bonds of the material world to achieve spiritual development. By taking action, or rajas, and having new experiences such as developing a spiritual practice, we can move to a more sattvic state of awareness. The siddhis—as you recall, these are accomplishments or abilities one can attain when approaching a greater sattvic state—are the direct result of that freedom. Moreover, they are signposts along the path of increasing divinity in your life.

Evaluating a Potential Teacher

In the Hindu and Tantra traditions, if an initiated teacher has given you the right to teach, then you are a teacher. In this instance, *initiated* means that he or she has received a direct transmission from another initiated teacher. Being given the right to teach means that an individual is empowered to share a body of knowledge or techniques with others. Most teachers are upa gurus like myself—householders—regular people seeking to lead an examined life that honors spirit and unveils the divinity in our world.

44

It is worth noting that, as a guru removes darkness, so can everything you encounter in life. Thus, my cat can be my guru—though despite some minor bloodletting rituals, he hasn't initiated me into anything. What he has provided me is companionship and love. And he *has* brought light into my world. If I were seeking to develop greater catness in my life, he would be well-suited to serve as my guru. However, as felinity is not my spiritual path, I need to look elsewhere to learn how to increase light in my very human life.

As mentioned earlier, the guru/chela relationship is often distorted, especially in the West, so it is important to find the proper teacher if you truly wish to achieve spiritual enlightenment and bliss through the practice of Tantra. One way to check the integrity of a teacher is to ask whether he seeks the independence of his students. If not, then it is quite possible the supposed guru is looking to take advantage of his students.

Other questions to ask and answers to look for when evaluating a potential teacher include:

When, where, and from whom did the teacher receive his training?
His training should be from an authentic, verifiable

source. A swami initiated in a particular Dasnami will have a notarized certificate and robes.

Does the teacher offer initiations?
If so, then the teacher has been initiated himself.

How does the teacher's daily spiritual practice affect his life? How has his spiritual practice changed his life?
The teacher's spiritual practice should have led him to spiritual development; his life should work for him; he should feel an increase of light and spirit. Be wary, though: If a teacher's story sounds too good to be true, it probably is. Traveling a spiritual path changes lives for better and for worse.

What does the teacher expect from you?
He may ask for your agreement to keep his teachings sacred, telling you that some teachings require study and preparation, and that it would be inappropriate for you to share them with someone who isn't prepared. He may tell you that he will present information for you to consider and examine. Be wary if he dictates actions or requires you to seek his advice before taking action.

How will you know when it's time to move on to another teacher?
The pace of spiritual development depends on the student.

Some people claim to have a disembodied person or a famous sat guru as their direct and personal teacher. Several of my friends have received such direct visitations, and their lives were significantly changed as a result. The effects are visible not only in them but also in their friends, family, and acquaintances.

Such occurrences are rare, though, and I would caution anyone who attempts to call out to specific dead people since doing so can be misleading and dangerous. Furthermore, a living teacher is much more accessible than a dead one. Not to mention the fact that students of live teachers are far less prone to the vagaries of fantasy and hearing only what they want to hear.

Another advantage of a living guru is that the journey we are on, from our first breath to our last, is a distinctly human journey. Whether we are human beings having a spiritual experience or spiritual beings having a human experience, our primary essence is human and we therefore have very human needs: oxygen for breathing, food and drink for sustenance, love. Furthermore, Tantra is about becoming as fully human as is humanly possible. A living, breathing teacher can offer insight, inspiration, and learning that is more directly assimilated than that from a discarnate one.

How Teachers Evaluate Potential Students

The guru is advised to observe the potential student for a year, looking for qualities such as: purity of soul, capacity for enjoyment, and desire for liberation. Teachers look for students who are pure in mind, whose senses are controlled, who are eager to do good to all beings, who are free from the concept of dualism, and who are dedicated to living at one with God. (Of course, if a teacher found a student with all of these qualities fully realized, the student wouldn't need the teacher.)

The above criteria may seem stringent—and that's because they are. Remember, the Tantras are the rites and rituals of spiritual growth, ultimately leading to unity with the

Divine. This is a path only for dedicated students, and requires great effort—especially today, millennia after Tantra's birth in a world very different from our own.

WORSHIP

The Sanskrit word for worship is *puja*. Puja can vary, but it is always done to honor an aspect of the Divine. Many people worship several aspects of God: Ganesha and Hanuman are auspicious

aspects of God for gay men. Ganesha (a man-god with an elephant head) breaks down barriers and blesses beginnings. Hanuman (a man-god with a monkey head) loved Rama, another male representation of God, so greatly that he gave Rama his heart, thereby ending his own life out of devotion to Rama.

50

Puja includes focus and intent to honor the specific aspect of God that you are addressing. It usually includes burning incense and making an offering. Furthermore, each aspect of God has a

specific mantra that must be repeated faithfully in the closest approximation to Sanskrit pronunciation you can make. (Imagine if, in English, you called out for "Dead" instead of "Dad," and you begin to see the importance.) Often there is an altar with an image of God to help focus your worship. Traditionally, such an altar would also include a Shiva lingam and possibly fresh flowers. Worship concludes with the gentle ringing of a bell.

In Tantra, worship should occur daily. If you wish to develop a swimmer's body, you must swim regularly. Similarly, if you wish to grow spiritually, you must practice daily. The word for daily spiritual practice is *sadhana*. This word is used in many religious practices other than Tantra, such as yoga.

In Tantra, daily practice may include mantra, pranayama (breathing techniques), kriya (breathing and visualization), puja, and bhakti (devotion). We also include lovemaking and erotic energies in our worship. In Part Two of this book, you will learn exercises that will allow you to join your spiritual and sexual practices, and that will help you incorporate this into your daily life.

Chapter Four
Venerating both male and female

In Tantra, we recognize that the world is comprised of many facets of the Divine. Similarly, humans have multiple facets. Two of these are what we call masculine and feminine. In the Tao they are known as *yang* (masculine) and *yin* (feminine). In Tantra, the male god Shiva and the female goddess Shakti best represent masculine and feminine. Not surprisingly, Shiva and Shakti can be combined into one figure, Ardhanarishvara. Ardhanarishvara is divided down the middle: Shiva has

the right side and Shakti the left. Like Ardhana-rishvara, everyone inherently has both genders and expresses these aspects of God throughout his or her life.

As gay men, I believe we have an advantage in not only understanding but also making present both the male (Shiva) and female (Shakti) aspects of the Divine. This is because, in contrast with our heterosexual brothers, it is easier for us to experiment with different roles of giving and receiving without threatening our identity. Gay sex roles can be fluid, and there is support in the gay community for a great variety of social and erotic experiences.

As gay men, we have also developed a strong goddess worship practice: drag. In drag, men transform themselves by calling forth their feminine side. The transformation often shows how closely related men and women are when the outer shell of clothes, hair, and makeup is altered to that of the other gender. Personally, I look like a very large version of my sister!

Doing drag has a very distinct impact, not only on the person in drag but also on those around her. Often that effect is one of creating a state of high energy. This is the presence of Shakti—the active female face of God, the magnetic forward-moving aspect—in contrast with Shiva, the meditating aspect. Shiva is like the still pond of deep contemplation, while Shakti is the wind that creates ripples and movement. Thus, through drag, gay men can experience the energy of the goddess.

56

There is no Sanskrit word that approximates our current understanding of the meaning of the word homosexual. One term, however, has an approximately similar meaning, especially in terms of drag and transgenderism: *hirja*.

The hirja were organized communities of men who lived in the female quarters of royal households. Their history is well-documented, and some groups survive even today. Hirjas express themselves socially as women and in bygone times were highly prized by royalty. It is likely that hirja communities have always included people who would today be termed homosexual, transvestite, hermaphrodite, eunuch, or transsexual. In Gujarat in northwest India, hirjas have worshiped their own patron saint, the goddess Bahucharaji. Bahucharaji is still venerated today with celebrations at every full moon. And it is still believed that dancing transvestites at traditional Hindu weddings bring good luck to a marriage. Consequently, modern hirja are often present as part of the ceremony.

At a very subtle level, both male and female energies course through each human body. It may help to think of these energies in terms of electrical poles. Like a magnet or a battery, every cell in the human body is comprised of positive and negative charges. (Even plants and minerals have inherent positive and negative poles.) Many people take the view that male energy is represented by the positive (expansive) pole, and female energy by the negative (receptive) pole.

Even though we may live with one pole more dominant than the other, both poles exist within the body, and with practice we can choose to make present one or the other pole more strongly at any given time. For men who love men, this is a great energetic and spiritual advantage.

It is an energetic advantage because we can choose to experience one, the other, or both of these electromagnetic poles. By crossing the social taboo against loving another man, we have the freedom to directly experience each of these ways of sexual expression—something very few hetero-only identified men can do.

It is a spiritual advantage because we have the opportunity to expand our understanding and compassion by playing with multiple roles. This then cultivates empathy: Once you've been there, you can feel for others in similar positions. Empathy expands your comfort zone, enabling you to better understand (meaning to "stand under" or "support") and connect with those around you.

When you read many contemporary Tantra books, you will encounter a strong heterosexual orthodoxy. The two poles, positive and negative (male and female), are represented as looking for their complement in each other, and are said to be incomplete without their opposite. But if, as discussed above, each of us contains both poles, how can we be incomplete?

To examine this paradox, let's use the analogy of magnets. You may remember from elementary school that magnets have positive and negative poles and that opposite poles attract. When the positive pole of one magnet was placed against the negative pole of another magnet, the electrical charge became grounded and the magnets clung together. On the other hand, when you placed two positive or two negative poles together, the magnets sent each other flying across the room. The coming together of two poles created a powerful energy.

From an exclusively heterosexual perspective, the maxim that opposites attract probably seems obvious. But it has never seemed obvious to me. In fact, as a child I actually enjoyed placing two positive magnetic poles together and watching the reaction. I liked the energy that was created.

From a purely scientific perspective, there is nothing inherently good or bad about either creating energy or grounding energy. This is knowledge that can be used in Tantra to further our spiritual understanding. As gay men we can bring our positive (male) energy together with another man's negative (female) energy to ground ourselves together. Or we can bring our positive poles together (quite literally) and create an energy that can quickly propel us into the realm of the gods.

Which brings us to the concept of *Kundalini*. Kundalini is a spiritual force that rests dormant approximately at the tip of the coccyx. It is a power and therefore referred to as a presence of Shakti, having a female personality trait. It is also viewed as a consciousness and therefore referred to as a presence of Shiva, having a male personality trait. Thus, Kundalini, which translates literally as "coiled serpent," expands both male and female consciousness as it rises. By receiving a well-placed touch from your partner, your Kundalini may become active and flow through you.

Kundalini is considered a primal energy but dormant. One of the goals of Tantra is to awaken this powerful, transformational energy. When your Kundalini rises, your life changes dramatically. It is like the difference between sleep and wakefulness. The experience is one of rising to the head, piercing the skull, and bringing dormant areas of the brain into blossom. Your creative intelligence flows more strongly, and supernormal mental capabilities may be activated. My experience at the river, described in the preface of this book, is a description of my first experience with active Kundalini.

60

As humans, we can do no better than to awaken our Kundalini. Kundalini is rocket fuel for our spiritual development. With practice, this energy can be directed with intention to areas of your body or life that you wish to transform. With even more practice, it can be directed to serve the greater good of mankind.

Happily, one of the best ways to awaken Kundalini is through sensual delight. Consequently, the practice of Tantra contains an erotic element that fans the flames of our spiritual growth. The remainder of this book contains discussion and exercises designed to help prepare you to awaken your Kundalini and experience spiritual and erotic bliss.

part two

Preparation
and Rituals

Parable—
a Tale of Two Temples

Many years ago, before words were written, there was a humble and pious monk. Out of bamboo and thatch he created a small temple for his family. The temple was very modest, and on the simple altar there was a place for one flower.

The valley in which the monk lived was abundant with a multitude of delightful flowers that grew on vines, bushes, and trees. These flowers decorated every inch of light they could find, reaching up to reflect the glory of the sun. Every morning the monk's niece went outside and found the most inspirational flower of the day, which she then hurried to bring to her uncle, who would consecrate it and place it on the altar, where it would bless the entire room.

As the humble and hardworking family came into the temple to meditate and to pray, they were moved by the gentle and rarified beauty of each flower—many of which released a blissful aroma that lifted their spirits. Every day, a different blossom touched their hearts, and the simple blossom temple became the center of the family's spiritual life.

By evening, though, the delicate blossom would have lost its radiance and be discarded.

One day a holy man came to this part of the world. Like the monk, he also was touched by the beauty of the flower-filled forest. And so he decided to stay for a while to repay the forest with worship for her kindness and the way she had helped him to smile again.

The monk was honored to have such a holy man nearby and invited him to pray and meditate with his family.

When the holy man was introduced to the temple and saw the single flower on the altar, though, he withdrew with great modesty so as not to hurt the monk's feelings. The holy man claimed that such a personal temple could only be for the dedicated family and that he preferred to worship directly in the forest.

The family was moved by the holy man's humility and gave him food, clothing, and shelter.

One morning soon after, the niece awoke quite ill, and everyone in the family gathered around to tend to her. The daily devotional offerings were suspended until after sunset, at which time the monk went into his temple and was accosted by a strong, unpleasant odor. As yesterday's flower had not been thrown out and replaced, it lay wilted, spent, and stinking up the temple. *How could something so beautiful, within a day, turn into an object of disgust?* The monk grabbed the vase containing the offending flower, stepped outside the temple, and, without seeing clearly, threw the faded flower and brackish water right onto the praying holy man.

The monk was horrified and ashamed by his action, and quickly ran to the holy man to apologize.

The holy man, dripping with this foul water, turned to the monk and invited him to step into the forest. They walked in silence for several minutes and came to a natural grotto in the side of a hill. There, orange tiger lilies clung to the moss and caught the last rays of a deep-pink sunset. The holy man kneeled, and the monk quickly dropped to his side.

As they knelt in the grotto, the monk became aware of a gentle and pervasive perfume that lifted his spirit like a gliding bird. The deep moist earth added to this perfume, deepening the fragrance. Then, from above, a clear vanilla aroma rode the gentle breeze, mixing in robust cedar, and the monk found himself suspended in bliss.

They stayed in the grotto on their knees until long after the sun had set and the moon had brightly risen. When it was time, the holy man and the monk arose with reverence and walked slowly back to the family home.

68

Upon returning, they received word that the niece had recovered and lay resting peacefully. There was some leftover rice and fish, and the monk and the holy man took their food and sat upon the doorstep.

After some time, the holy man spoke: "Today, we were in two temples."

The monk was surprised, as he knew they had been only in his family's temple.

The holy man then rose, and the monk followed him to a tree. "Here," the holy man said "is another temple." They walked a few more paces, coming to a night-blooming vine. "Here," said the holy man, "is yet another temple."

The holy man then asked the monk what *he* saw.

"A flower, " answered the monk.

"What does it take to be a flower?" asked the holy man.

The monk paused and looked at the silky petals, the stamen, and the pollen stains left by a messy bee. He stepped closer in the filtered moonlight to smell. Smelling gave him no clue.

"Can the flower exist without its roots?" the holy man asked. "Can the flower exist without soil, or water, or air, or its leaves? Can it exist without bees or ants?" Then he asked, "Is the flower all of these things, or just the pretty end of its branch?"

And finally the monk understood that he must allow himself to recognize all of the beauty of life—the seed, the roots, the branches and leaves, the petals, even the messy dirt and bugs, for all of those elements contribute to the beauty of the flower. The existence of the bloom requires every element present; none is better or worse than the other.

How many times in life do we try to separate out the *pure* elements and by doing so cut off our very power and life source? Many religions and belief systems require their adherents and followers to lead lives of *purity* of diet, thought, and erotic expression. By pursuing paths of purity, individuals cut themselves off at the stem and can then only wilt. It is much more rewarding to realize that all aspects of our life, even the unattractive parts, are necessary for our survival. Our human bodies require that we take in food, liquid, and air. We then excrete or expel the unused parts once we have extracted nourishment from the materials. Like the flower in this parable, we need all of life's elements to flourish.

Chapter Five
breathing

Breathing is largely an unconscious act. It happens without ceasing, usually without our will or knowledge, until we take our final breath. Consequently, our experience of life is constantly riding on the ebb and flow of air as we inhale and exhale. Air, through breathing, is our primary connection with the world around us.

When we breathe we take in oxygen and other gases and infuse our blood supply with elements vital for life, most notably oxygen. The process is complex: Basically, though, there is an exchange in the alveolar sac where the airborne gases move into our bloodstream and are then carried to the heart, which pumps blood throughout the body via a system of arteries. Imagine now that the air you inhaled as you were reading the first paragraph on breathing is now circulating through your body.

Similarly, our veins carry waste from our cells—including leftover "air"—to the lungs to be expelled when we exhale. Exhalation rids the body of gaseous elements that are not or are no longer useful to us. This cycle of infusing our bloodstream with oxygen and expelling useless gases—breathing—is one of the bases of our existence.

It is possible, of course, to not breathe for short periods of time. Sometimes this happens spontaneously, usually when we are feeling fear or anxiety. A good example is a tense moment in a thrilling film. The reason for this is that when we breathe we expand our experience of all parts of life, including feelings. When we spontaneously hold our breath, we are usually unconsciously trying to minimize an uncomfortable feeling. Thus, in the thriller movie we hold our breath because we are experiencing fear. Not breathing is a way to manage that fear. This involuntary response is quite common. I can remember once before a performance that my stage fright was so great that I was inhaling with short, frequent puffs and couldn't get the air I needed into my lungs. I was afraid—and scared of being afraid. I did not wish to expand those negative feelings and therefore experienced difficulty breathing.

Some people live in constant fear and therefore breathe minimally. Over time, this reflex can become a habit—a destructive habit. By breathing less, you live less, missing out on the full experience of the world around you.

Remember: Tantra is all about *expansion,* the deepening of experience. This means deepening what we at a superficial level would consider either good or bad experiences.

Prana

In Tantra we describe the life force as *prana.* There are several types of prana, but for our purposes prana is similar to the Chinese *chi* or Japanese *ki.* It surrounds the body. It is often easiest to visualize prana as entering the body through breathing. Much of what we do in Tantra involves learning how to master prana. Thus, proper breath technique is the most basic tool of Tantra.

Breath Technique Exercises

Preparing yourself for Tantra takes time, effort, and energy. The exercises presented below (both in this chapter and throughout the remainder of the book) are designed to increase your experience of the Divine. It is important to note that they are presented sequentially and that skipping to the end will not produce the ecstatic and erotic bliss you desire. That takes preparation. Skipping to the final chapter would be akin to a new bicycle owner attempting to race the Tour de France.

Tantric lovemaking, in particular, requires preparation. Tantric lovemaking usually takes place over an extended period of time. (However, my great colleague Umeshanand has reminded me of Lysbeth's tantric maxim: A Tantric lover is able to satisfy his partner with a mere embrace.) Working from a pleasure principle, then, you will want to increase your lung power and stamina.

Proper preparation and practice, beginning with breathing, will equip you and strengthen you so you can handle ever-increasing states of bliss. I suggest that if you are serious about Tantra, you should now start to set aside a specific period of time each day to perform the necessary exercises.

BASIC BREATHING

In Tantra, we start with the breath and stay with the breath to increase divinity in our lives. Through breath practice, we learn that inhaling is like a switch we can use to turn on divinity. By breathing more and breathing more consciously, we expand our world, connecting on a more profound level with creation. Even when we feel less than the Beauty of the Divine, we can easily reconnect once we've developed a breath-prana pathway.

To begin, breathe through your nostrils only. As you focus on the breath entering and exiting the nostrils, notice if the breath moves more easily through one nostril. Just make a mental note of it. Now imagine the volume of air in front of your body that you will be inhaling. How far does it extend? Imagine that this volume of air is prana and that it is the color of sparkling gold. With your next inhalation, bring these golden sparkles into your lungs.

If your mind wanders or you lose concentration, bring your focus back to your nostrils. Pay attention to all the details of breathing. Feel the air moving back and forth. Envision the intensity of the golden color of the prana you are breathing. Feel how your intercostal (rib) muscles, your diaphragm, and your back and belly relate. Does your neck expand? Is your tongue relaxed? Your eyes? Exploring the minute details of each breath will deepen your experience of divine bliss.

The Backward *Ah*

For this exercise, first make the sound *ah* as in *fah*ther. Holding the shape in your mouth and

throat, inhale through the *ah* position. As you inhale, see how far you can open your mouth and throat while maintaining the *ah* position and keeping your tongue relaxed.

Now listen. As you inhale, are you doing it silently? If not, see what it takes to make the inhalation in this open mouth and throat position imperceptible.

When you have accomplished this, with one hand make a hollow fist and bring it to your lips. Rapidly inhale with a backward *ah,* and then forcefully exhale through your fist, as if you are blowing up a small paper bag. Repeat this at least seven times.

When you become comfortable with the Backward Ah it is time to move on to the Golden Straw Exercises.

Golden Straw Exercise 1

For the first Golden Straw Exercise, assume a comfortable sitting position in an environment where you will be undisturbed. Allow your eyelids to rest like a shade drawn partway so that you can see slightly through the bottom of your eyes. Your tongue should be asleep, lying comfortably in the internal space of your jaw. Inhale through your nose, hold your breath for a few moments, and allow yourself to become calm and steady, then exhale gently. Visualize the golden life force around you. After several breaths, imagine a long tube shaped like a straw that goes from your nostrils to your sacrum at the base of your spine. With your next inhalation, imagine the golden prana moving through this straw to your sacrum. As you exhale, see it moving up and out of your nostrils.

Take a few moments to check in with how this feels. Move your head and neck to find the optimum position—the one that gives you the most volume of air. Now check in with your shoulders, arms, and back. How can you adjust your posture, using ease and volume of breath as the organizing principles? Take time to notice how you feel after each adjustment.

Once you have found the posture that works best for you, I recommend that you set a timer and breathe this way, starting with two minutes and gradually building to 10 minutes over the course of several weeks. Do this daily, preferably not directly after a meal and definitely not after drinking alcohol. To not do these exercises daily will yield little. Daily practice will anchor them.

Seven consecutive days of practicing this exercise for 10 minutes will prepare you for the next level of Golden Straw.

Golden Straw Exercise 2

After you have practiced the first Golden Straw Exercise for at least seven consecutive days, make this modification: Wake the tongue up. This is accomplished by touching the tip of your tongue to the roof of your mouth at the corner where the hard palate turns downward. To find this spot, run your tongue from behind your two upper front teeth upward until the tissue flattens onto the roof of your mouth. With the tongue in this position, perform the Golden Straw Exercise as described above. Visualize the golden life force around you. Then, seated in your optimum posture, inhale, imagining the golden prana traveling down a long tube that runs from your nostrils to your sacrum. Hold the breath for a few moments, allowing yourself to feel calm and peaceful, and then exhale along the same path through the nose. Practice this exercise for 10 minutes for at least seven consecutive days before moving to the next exercise.

Golden Straw Exercise 3

After you have practiced the second Golden Straw Exercise for at least seven consecutive days, you are ready to move on to Exercise 3. Position yourself as you did with Exercise 2, including the position of your tongue. Then, rather than inhaling through your nose, inhale through your mouth. Imagine the golden prana traveling down a long tube that runs from your mouth to your sacrum. Hold the breath for a few moments, allowing yourself to feel calm and peaceful, and then exhale gently. Use the backward *ah* position when you exhale, but with the tongue elevated and touching the roof of the mouth. Practice this exercise for at least 10 minutes for at least seven consecutive days before moving to the next exercise.

Golden Straw Exercise 4

This exercise is the same as Exercise 3, except it's done with a partner. Sit face to face in a spider-legs position: Your partner's left leg should be under your right knee, and your left leg should be under his right knee. Support each other's back with your hands and allow your foreheads to touch. When you begin, match your breathing, inhaling and exhaling at the same time. Once you have experienced that, alternate your breathing. As you inhale, he exhales; as you exhale, he inhales. Be aware of both your life force and the life force of your partner. Observe how the two techniques differ and feel which approach deepens your experience the most.

Chapter Six
posture and movement

Proper posture and ease of movement are essential to the practice of Tantra. This is because our posture and how we move are directly related to how we approach and relate to the world.

As an example, allow yourself to move into a depressed posture right now as you are reading this. Where do you feel your weight? Where are the resting points on your body for the weight of your head, torso, legs, and feet? How well-prepared are you to move or take action from this position? Let the depressed posture take hold and then venture out into public. Who looks at you? What is in their eyes if and when they look at you?

Now imagine yourself after the most wonderful, awe-inspiring, ecstatic erotic union. Allow your body to move into these new feelings so you are filled with that beauty in every cell. Now where does your head rest? Your torso, legs, and feet? Is your body ready to move, take action? Carry this attitude with you into public, and see how differently people react to you.

The fact is, the human body and the emotions are related. We can therefore effect change from both directions: working internally so that our emotional state informs the body and working externally so that the body informs our emotions.

The exercises in this chapter are designed to create postures that properly align the body, leading to ease of movement and greater feelings of bliss and the Divine.

The human body has a very interesting mechanism where we remember at a cellular level. This memory serves to maintain the status quo and gives us a feeling of safety. This creates a posture "home zone" in which you feel most comfortable.

While you may feel most comfortable in your home zone, it also fences you in. As part of the expansion process of Tantra, however, you can actively and successfully expand your home zone to include more of the human endeavor. You still feel safe in your expanded home zone, but are not as fenced in and therefore more open to new experience and spiritual growth.

In traditional Tantra the student is often encouraged to knock down these imaginary fences and to expand this safety zone in order to grow spiritually. There is a parallel in the S/M community, where men are lead to greater levels of intensity and physicality by experienced tops. Like the leather community, Tantra prizes safety, sanity, and consensual participation.

Expanding your home zone can be a difficult process. If your primary attitude has been one of depression, your body assumes a depressed posture, which eventually becomes your home zone— the posture in which you are most comfortable (because it is familiar, not because it is physically comfortable).

Along this path of human endeavor our emotional state sometimes gets stuck. In cases like this a qualified, licensed mental health practitioner is the best resource. In this book I will not attempt to enter the world of psychotherapy. If you feel this is one of your next steps, I recommend you seek professional counseling.

In this chapter we will focus on postures that align our bodies to create greater feelings of bliss and awareness of the divine.

GRAVITY

Ordinary life is lived within the pull of gravity; it governs the ebb and flow of the tides as well as the change of seasons. Advanced Tantric practices can lead to a suspension of gravity, where meditation leads to levitation. But this is reserved for Olympian Tantrikas and is not a usual goal for those of us simply looking to lead an examined life of ever-increasing Divinity. Therefore, we all must contend with gravity. (So must the levitators, incidentally.)

Since gravity is an omnipresent force in our lives, it is logical to align the mechanics of the body with its pull, aiming for states of posture and being that are either supported by gravity or minimize its constant downward pull.

Standing, sitting, or reclining with poor posture is known as misalignment. Anyone who has used an external computer mouse for any length of time has experienced misalignment. People who experience this on a continual basis for an extended period of time sometimes develop an ache known as "mouse shoulder." Mouse shoulder is an example of body noise.

Likewise, as people drive cars, watch movies, or nap on the couch, they place themselves in constant misalignment. For example, since I am tall and frequently travel, I am often forced to mold my long body into an "average"-size seat on airplane or in a car or train. Similarly, if you are *below* "average" size, whatever the seat designers have determined that to be, you also experience misalignment.

Because your body remembers what is familiar and uses that to create your safety zone—your home posture—you gradually come to know yourself only in misaligned postures. This creates body noise that makes it all the more difficult to hear your authentic self. It is a little like trying to watch television or read while living next to an elevated train track. It is still possible to experience the authentic self, but that requires much more concentration than it normally would. Consequently, eliminating body noise by improving one's posture is highly recommended for those studying Tantra.

The following exercises are designed to improve posture and decrease body noise.

Skeletal Alignment Or, Heels-Hips-Shoulders

To begin, stand with your feet shoulder-width apart and your toes pointing directly in front of you. Rock forward and back over your heels. Find where your weight falls through your legs and onto your heels. Next, rock forward and back to find the point where the weight of your hips falls directly through your legs (with your knees very slightly bent), entering the floor beneath your heels. Now your lower body is in proper alignment.

To align your upper body, stand with your lower body in proper alignment and rock your torso until you find the point where your shoulders line up over your hips (that are over your heels). From this position, allow your head to float upward while your jaw stays relaxed. This lengthens the back of your neck, where the vertebral column enters your skull.

Now you are in your baseline posture. From this position you can move in many directions without having to make corrections for structural imbalances. This posture also has great "presence." If you observe charismatic leaders, actors, and other performers, you will notice that they nearly always use this baseline posture. Though this posture may be new to you and in the beginning awkward, I recommend highly that you integrate it into your daily life as much as possible—while waiting in line, for example. Soon enough, this baseline posture will become your home posture. You will feel comfortable in it, and your body noise will be greatly reduced.

MOVEMENT

We are constantly in motion, even while we sleep: Our hearts beat, and cells slough off and die, to be replaced by younger, more virile cells; we breathe in oxygen and expel waste through our lungs. Our very complex bodies are never still. Likewise, when we are awake, do we move with ease, speed, and certainty? Are your movements in harmony with the great flow of life, or do you feel sometimes as if you are swimming upstream, fighting your environment? Do your movements support your goals?

There is a gentleman whom I've observed for more than 15 years running through my neighborhood. Instead of flowing through the air, as though it supported him or helped propel him forward, he runs as if he were bucking a great wind, with great tension and exertion as he exercises his body. I can only wonder what drives him to punish himself this way. How I admire the other runners, whose inner radiance beams through them as they achieve greater speeds and distances in a loving and understanding relationship with their bodies.

Tantra uses the mundane as a way to learn deep spiritual truths. By focusing on the process of life-giving breath, we begin to transform ourselves literally from the inside out. By focusing on posture and mechanical alignment, we learn to work with the body to reduce pain and noise as well as come into greater harmony with our environment.

By focusing on movement, we combine breath, inner transformation, and our physical bodies to support us in the ebb and flow of life. If we work with constant awareness on these three elements (breath, posture, and movement) as paths to increase Divinity in our lives, we will yield great results.

To integrate this baseline posture with walking, pay attention to your back stride. The back stride is how your heel lifts off the ground when you walk. Typically with each step, your foot lands first with the heel and the weight rolls to the ball of your foot as you move, thereby lifting your heel. Now, with this awareness, allow the ball of your foot to flop down like a sloppy slipper and shift your awareness to the back stride—the part of the movement where your heel lifts off the ground. Now notice, do your knees track directly in front of you? Do your toes track along with your knees, directly in front of you? Are your upper legs moving freely and directly forward? Does your upper torso rest in the bowl of your pelvis, with your shoulders, neck, and head floating on top?

As you make modifications, what happens to the speed of your gait? My test is asking myself how much I experience the effortlessness of being in the flow. When my body and movements are in harmony with each other, I reduce my level of body noise and aches and pains, therefore giving myself more space to recognize the eternal ebb and flow in which I exist. It is important to note that the only two elements we are all given in equal measure are time and gravity.

We all have different capacities for movement due to our height, weight, age, and the effects of gravity on the human body over time. Certain conditions, such as scoliosis, may prevent you from having the same experience as that of a 19-year-old Olympic gymnast. By working with these principles, however, you can achieve your greatest potential: to go as far as you can, given who you are and how you use what you have.

SITTING

We weren't born to sit, which is why sitting properly is so problematic for many of us. In general, find a way to sit so that your hips are slightly higher than your knees. If you meditate, you must sit on a cushion. The longer your meditation sessions, the higher the cushion needs to be (a trick taught to me by a Buddhist.) Also, sit so that the weight of your torso falls down and rests on your "sitz" bones that compose the ischial tuberosity of your pelvis. When you sit this way, it engages your abdominal matrix and removes stress from your back. It also opens the pelvic bowl to make room for your genitals—they will thank you for this. Remember, even resting or reclining puts stress on your back, which is ill-designed for the purpose.

ROLFING AND FELDENKRAIS

For individuals with posture issues that can't be corrected with simple exercise such as those described above, there are other options. In particular, two physical therapy modalities can help you achieve deep postural changes: Rolfing (also known as Structural Integration) and Feldenkrais (also known as Functional Integration).

Rolfing was developed by Ida Rolf after she examined the physiological relationship between bones, muscles, ligaments, and the myofacial connective tissue. She invented a method of bodywork that, when performed over a period of 10 weeks, returns the body to a natural baseline posture.

Feldenkrais was developed by Moshe Feldenkrais. It is an approach similar to Rolfing and is designed to return the body to a natural, pain-free posture. Feldenkrais involves repetitive exercises that isolate specific muscle groups and change the organization of those structures. Like Rolfing, Feldenkrais works at the cellular memory level to create physiological changes.

Rolfing is faster but requires you to be mostly passive (it's done to you). Feldenkrais is slower, but you learn exercises to do on your own and therefore gain independence from the practitioner. If these options interest you, resources for information on both Rolfing and Feldenkrais are listed in the resource section at the end of this book.

Chapter Seven
developing your midsection

Your midsection is very important in Tantra, as it forms the physical and energetic connections between your genitals and your heart. The human body is already hardwired for Tantra—all we need to do is develop expertise in arousing and directing the flows in and around us. To do this, we'll explore our abdominals, the physiology of the genitals, and the spiritual significance of ejaculate.

ABDOMINALS

Who doesn't like seeing a firm set of abs? I believe gay men are particularly aroused by taut abs—especially when they are worked to the point of vascularity—because the four muscle layers of our abdomen are the same as the muscles that make up the shaft of the penis. Hard abs, therefore, are just an extension of a hard cock.

While developing in the womb, the penis of a male fetus descends but doesn't penetrate the abdominal wall; rather, it remains covered by the abdominal wall but stretches it, as if stretching four layers of latex. As an adult, you'll find that strengthening your abdominal matrix has the benefit of helping create stronger, longer-lasting erections and decreasing the risk of premature ejaculation.

94

By conditioning your abdominal layers, you'll gain greater back support as well as more genital strength. The following exercises focus on strengthening both the deepest abdominal layer as well as the muscles that support erections. In addition, they'll help tone your waist and midsection.

The body, muscles, and tendons all have an inherent memory. Transformation means changing your form. Your muscles have stored memories for many years, after having learned dutifully based on how you move and use them. Your current physical shape is your most comfortable posture and form. Therefore, change means having to unlearn your body's current form and reinforce the new desirable form. The good news is that our muscles have a keen memory for recent input. This means you can flood your muscle memory banks with new information, reinforce that information with repetition, and enjoy the results.

Transformation is hard work, but the satisfaction of witnessing your results is worth all the effort, time, and energy.

Fourth-Layer Exercise

Lie on your back with your feet flat on the floor and your knees raised. Your arms should be resting at your sides. Begin by releasing most of the air in your lungs as you contract your abdominals. Keep the air passages open to allow the remaining air to exit as necessary. Do not force the air passageways shut after exhaling. Keep your throat relaxed and open at all times. As you do this, see how far you can push your belly button into your spine. Your back should be flat against the floor.

With the air blown out and your belly button as close to your spine as possible, first lift your right knee to your chest, then set it down. Once your right foot is on the floor, lift your left knee and set it down likewise. With both feet on the ground, inhale, extending your belly to the sky, then exhale forcefully, always pushing your belly button to your spine. Now lift your left arm and hand over your head and return them to your side, followed by your right arm and hand over your head, then returned to your side. Inhale and exhale again.

Now we can combine the movements for the exercise. Inhale fully, belly to sky, and exhale forcefully, belly button to spine. Lift your right knee and left hand simultaneously, then set them down simultaneously. With your air still out, lift your left knee and right hand at the same time, then return to the starting position. Inhale. Work until you can do seven sets (one combination of right knee-left hand and left knee-right hand is one set) all in one breath.

Men of all fitness levels can do this abdominal exercise. Please modify it to your beginning stage and then work to increase the intensity (degree of contraction and flection.) This exercise works the transversus abdominis muscle group that runs from your groin to your rib cage.

Beginners should start with one 10-minute set daily, then work up to two 10-minute sets if possible. For more advanced practitioners, slow down your movements and add ankle weights and a light dumbbell for your hands. Always focus your movement on the flection and extension of the abdominal muscles by keeping your belly button pressed to your spine and then extended at the inhale.

Cock Push-ups: Level I

This exercise creates firmer and longer-lasting erections. When your penis is semierect, use muscle contractions to make your cock bob up and down in front of you. Isolate your hips and back so that solely the muscles that control your cock's functions of urination and ejaculation cause the movement.

Many men find viewing their swelling member erotic, so practice this one in front of a mirror. As you get harder, you will find it takes more effort to lift the penis with just your musculature—kind of like adding weights to a barbell. To gain the greatest benefit from this exercise, stimulate yourself only to a semierect state.

Cock Push-ups: Level II

To strengthen the muscles of your penis even more, begin to add weights, just like in the gym. Start lightly at first by wrapping a small dry washcloth around your penis. As you gain strength, wet the washcloth to increase the weight. Don't get greedy; begin with modest weights and practice five minutes daily, perhaps after showering or bathing when you are relaxed and comfortable.

Root Lock

You can practice the root lock anywhere, since it's a simple closing and opening of the anus, like a gentle inward and upward pull. As you develop proficiency with the root lock, play with it to see if you can contract just the perineum, the area between the scrotum and the anus.

Beginning Root Lock

In any sitting position, you can practice the root lock by gently pulling the outer anal sphincter inward and upward. It feels like you're preventing gas from passing. Begin by gently contracting and relaxing those muscles. As you gain more control, inhale, retain your breath, and rapidly contract and release 20 times before exhaling. Repeat this cycle nine times. Every day add 10 repetitions to your nine cycles until you reach 60. Then do just one cycle (one cycle is one retained breath) of 60, 70, 80, and 90 until you reach 108 comfortably without straining.

Advanced Root Lock

Lie on your back with your knees to the ceiling. Imagine a small flower. In your mind, gently tap this flower onto your perineum. As you do this in your mind, allow your perineum to react by gently flinching. Make the motion or reaction ever smaller yet distinct enough to be a physical stimulation. As in the beginning exercise, make your contractions while retaining your breath.

The root lock is a technique we use to strengthen and seal our energetic container. There are times when we need energies to flow through us, so we wouldn't use it at those times. Later you will see how to incorporate the root lock into your erotic practice.

EJACULATION

Most men have an orgasm when they ejaculate, and this single event becomes the central drive of their sexual life. With practice we can learn to have multiple orgasms that don't include ejaculation. Prolonging ejaculation is generally a tool used to extend lovemaking sessions. Some Tantric practices require heightened states of arousal that occur over time. And because the party is usually over after ejaculation, learning to manage ejaculation is a tool that can help us.

Some Eastern schools teach the avoidance of

ejaculation and work with students to minimize it, if not eliminate it altogether. In Tantra nothing is forbidden, so there's no bias for or against ejaculation or orgasm. In Tantra, the power of the ejaculate, which many schools want to conserve, is a psychic power, like prana or *chi.* Confusing the power directly with the ejaculate is like confusing prana with air.

There's a parallel between the rising of semen through an erection and the experience of spiritual awakening. To ejaculate takes great force. You mix semen with ejaculate fluid and then pump it to a holding tank and finally release it out the head of the penis, usually in a display of fireworks. To ejaculate requires flection of the back, gluts, abdominals, and quadriceps in the legs. In fact, some men enjoy flexing many of their muscles all at once to create one great come-pumping piston.

From a spiritual perspective, it also takes great force to transcend our normal everyday waking consciousness and to reach Divine heights of ecstasy. The rise of the Kundalini through the spine, piercing the brain and blasting through the skull, is very similar to the rise of semen through an erect penis, blasting out and spreading your seed.

Chapter Eight
meditation

There's a great body of books and research on meditation. Many spiritual traditions encourage meditative contemplation of the Divine. Much of what we call ceremony or sacred space has a meditative quality about it. These qualities are usually reverence, quiet, listening, stillness, and time.

REVERENCE

Usually, we relearn spiritual qualities by recognizing a certain sacred space that is different from mundane life. A primary quality of sacred space is reverence for the Divine. By sitting or moving reverentially, we change our attitude and how we hold ourselves. This change signals the energies of the Divine that surround us and make up our environment; it tells the Divine that we are ready—ready to deepen our relationship with the Divine.

102

QUIET

In the beginning stages, it is beneficial to find a peaceful, quiet, undisturbed place to meditate. Locking the door and turning off the phones show the Divine that you are serious about creating space where you can explore this intimate connection with God.

LISTENING

There are indeed times to talk to God. And there are times to listen to God. I would venture that is what the continual flow of mind chatter is anyway: reporting our feelings, thoughts, and experiences. In meditation, we set aside space to allow our inner television reportage to take a commercial break. We give our mind a chance to relax and open the self to deeper and greater understanding.

As it is difficult to simultaneously speak and hear, meditation gives us a tool to be able to listen more acutely and integrate this new information more fundamentally into our lives.

STILLNESS

"Still waters run deep" is an old saying that is not without value when you are beginning to learn meditation techniques. During the early stages, a still and undisturbed setting will help you focus your mind, body, and spirit into a receptive state. Through meditation we each become a receptacle for God. Through meditation we each can build a strong container to hold powerful, transformative energies. With practice, we loose the sense of *doing* meditation and enter the realm of simply *being*.

TIME

Time: The fourth dimension. After meditating, many people report an onion peel-like experience of having uncovered a multiplicity of layers, each deeper than the one before. The experience can truly be likened to peeling a white onion, since during meditation you go into greater states of transparency as you approach the center. It's best to start slowly, but over time you will go deeper and attain greater depths of consciousness faster. Remember there is always farther to travel.

GOALS

Different schools present different agendas or goals for meditation. For some, the meditative space is a large void, a place of "no-thing." My experiences have been different. I present them here for your consideration, though yours may be very different and equally valid.

The results and fruits of my practice of meditation have been the opposite of nothing. In meditation, doors to abundantly rich worlds have opened up for me. Instead of experiencing a void or emptiness, I have reached worlds beyond language, resplendent with images and color. The river vision I shared at the beginning of this book is an example of what I experienced during one of my meditations.

TYPES OF MEDITATION

BASIC MEDITATION

This is an easy beginning-meditation exercise. Find a time, place, and setting where you will be undisturbed. Make sure your phones are switched off and your pets or children are well taken care of so that you won't have to attend to their needs. It might be best to meditate either when you get up in the morning, before a meal or before going to sleep. It's best to avoid meditating on a full stomach, after drinking alcohol, or after taking mind-altering substances.

Meditation has a beginning, a middle, and an end. To start, set a timer so that you can release your mind from needing to keep track of seconds and minutes. While you may want to meditate before going to sleep, I recommend that you not use meditation as a method to *fall* asleep. After completing your meditation, you can then prepare yourself for sleep.

Find a comfortable sitting position, one in which your back is straight and your head floats effortlessly over your torso. If you're sitting in a chair and using the back support is most comfortable for you, then do that to begin. Over time see if you can graduate to sitting on the front edge of the seat of the chair, so that the weight of your torso rests on your "sitz" bones.

Rest your arms on top of your thighs. In more advanced practices, we connect different fingers for different effects. If you feel so moved, connect the tips of each of your fingers of your right and left hands with its exact counterpart: thumb to thumb, forefinger to forefinger, and so forth. Allow them to touch as lightly as possible. Keep your feet flat on the floor and your legs uncrossed. Allow your breathing to be steady and relaxed. Breathe through your nose and close your eyes.

As you begin, many thoughts and feelings will come to your attention. Know that you will remember everything that is important. Know that it will come back to you at an appropriate time. Sometimes it helps to give the mind a job to do to help us in early phases of meditation. Here are two minor tasks: (1) Think the sound *om*. Make no sound; just hear *om* internally as you inhale and exhale. (2) Allow yourself to deepen every detail of your meditation. Notice how you can release your shoulders and, with more relaxation, how your meditation deepens. Keep noticing more and more details until the meditative experience becomes more fulfilling than the mind's discovery of it.

While we think of meditation as a solo experience, in Tantra we combine yogic techniques from different disciplines to forward our growth. Meditation is one of these techniques, along with breathing (pranayama), directing energy (prana), and learning how to apply esoteric or subtle bodies during our erotic and sexual experiences.

PRANA

Developing a calm meditative practice will give you a baseline upon which you can build your Tantra practice. Bringing awareness to the flow of prana in you and between you and your partner is another basic building block. Use this warm-up daily to familiarize yourself with prana and to anchor it to your body.

Prana Warm-Up

Energize your hands by vigorously rubbing your palms together for one minute. Next, contract your fingers into the palms of your hands and flick them open, as though you were going to flick water from your fingernails as far as possible. Do this rapidly with your fingers for three minutes, spending one minute in each of these three positions: first, flick your fingers with your palms facing downward to the earth; next, flick your fingers with your palms turned upward to the sky; and finally, flick your fingers directly in front of you.

Now take the thumb of your right hand and press it deeply into the palm of the left for 30 seconds. Do the same with your left thumb in the center of the right palm.

Bring your hands in front of you with your palms facing together, as though you were holding a large egg. Keep your fingers semirelaxed. We feel prana the most when we are in a state of alert relaxation, calm and focused. What do you feel in your palms?

Allow your eyelids to gently close halfway; this is known as the hanging shade position. Bring your awareness to the space between your palms. Gently allow your hands to move so that you maintain a sense of electromagnetic connection between your palms. How far can you expand this energetic egg you are holding? At what point do you lose your sense of connection? Experiment by tensing your fingers. What does that do to your sensation of prana? What happens when you tense your forearms?

Which position brings you the greatest feeling between your palms? That position is the correct one for you.

Chapter Nine
The launching pad

Everything up to this point has explained the historical and technical underpinnings of Tantra for gay men. Now we are ready to begin to combine different components and focus our attention on the body-based, Eros-centered spiritual pursuit that is Tantra. But first we need to consider one more aspect, and then you will learn how to create a Tantra session for yourself or together with your partner.

DEVOTION

Devotion is the emotional quality of reverence and love. It can be quiet and reflective or loud and boisterous. Devotion is the key to opening the heartfelt feelings of deep love that lead to the path of ever-increasing oneness with the All. In Tantra, devotion can be to your own inner divinity or a specific deity or the presence of God in your beloved. In Tantra, we view everything as a reflection of the Divine. Therefore, we can worship at the altar of our beloved: his body.

I believe this is what we are doing anyway, though usually without the awareness of how erotic worship is a portal to greater realms of spirituality. Heterosexuals can miss the contact point of the erotic with the Divine by justifying their acts as biological imperatives. For gay men, when we dig deeply we find how our sexuality creates high states of energy that connect us profoundly to spirit. If this interests you, you may find the section on creating a Tantra session most enlightening.

The tactile techniques of Tantra and the spirit of devotion deepen your connection and your intimacy. The following is a simple and powerful exercise to help you experience your beloved's inner spirituality.

Sit close, facing each other knee to knee. Gently hold hands and softly gaze into your partner's left eye. Sit in silence like this for at least 10 minutes, remaining aware of your thoughts, feelings, impressions, and desires. Can you let your beloved look deeper into you? Can you risk sharing your deepest, most precious self with him?

Now, with this knowledge and experience of your partner's divinity, how differently will you approach him in daily life? In lovemaking? Will your

110

lovemaking be down 'n' dirty warrior sex, or will you erotically finger the iridescent wings of God?

Unlocking devotion during your lovemaking and in your life as a whole strengthens the bonds between you and your beloved. The Greeks knew this. In the 4th century BCE, their special military forces, the Sacred Band of Thebes, were pairs of lovers. The commanders of the military knew

these men would fight ferociously to protect the object of their love and devotion: their beloved who was fighting alongside them.

Sometimes we use words of the spirit to describe sexual and erotic inspiration—for example,

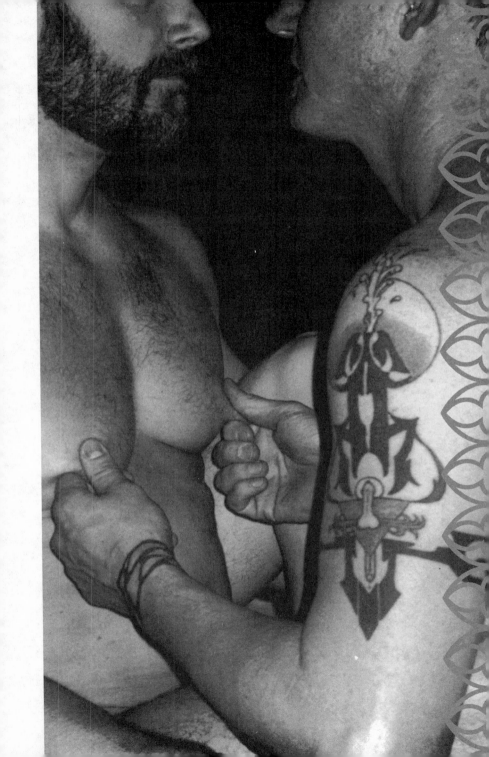

114

"Oh, God!"—uttered at the height of ecstasy. Sometimes we describe sexual inspiration in terms of a god, as in the Greek god Adonis. Some men have a difficult time with the concept of erotic/spiritual devotion, especially since much of our religious training runs counter to combining sex and spirituality. In addition, when we discover the erotic doorway to the Divine, power shifts from institution-based religion to personal spiritual revelation. Ultimately, this shift in power threatens the religious and political matrix in which we live.

We've explored how breath, like the nucleus of our cells, is the center of Tantric practice. We use breath to expand our experience by developing a creative working relationship with prana (our life force). By paying attention to posture and how we organize the structure and function of the body, we can decrease the stresses of life that create noise. This body noise takes up valuable energy and mental space, creating suffering and diminishing the divine qualities of daily life. From an electromagnetic perspective we've seen how currents flow in and through the body, and with practice these currents can be directed at will. The emotional orientation of devotion is the final major ingredient in our Tantric pantry.

CREATING YOUR TANTRIC SESSION
PREPARATION

Before you create your first Tantric rocket-launching session, you need to feel well-grounded in the breathing, midsection toning, and prana exercises. Developing a stronger midsection from sternum to foreskin (for those lucky enough to have one) will also deepen your experience.

Just as a space shuttle departure is never a spontaneous event, neither should your Tantric session be. So, in planning your session with your beloved, set aside a time and place where you both will feel relaxed and energized and won't be interrupted. Even if you're creating a solo session, follow each of these steps, adapting them to your personal tastes and desires.

SETTING

Find a space separate from your sleeping quarters that you can define as sacred. Begin by creating an altar together that includes talismans and objects that lift both your spirits toward the Divine. I suggest you avoid including statues of gods or goddesses unless you have a direct and personal relationship with these deities already.

Your setting is better simple than cluttered, better authentic than elaborate, better feeling-based than based on impressive mental constructs. I also recommend including at least a candle, and if you like incense, choose one with a sweet, pleasing fragrance.

116

Preset your launching pad with everything you'll need: pillows, sheets, towels, lube, toys, tissues, music, water, etc. Then prepare yourself. You may at times wish to spend time alone, gathering your feelings separately before coming together. You may also want to spend time preparing each other by shaving each other, bathing together, or applying oil or lotion to each other. Or you may feel moved to ask your beloved to do something for you—perhaps a request you've never made, such as a new way of sharing your eroticism with each other. If you have special clothes or jewelry that make you feel most prepared for the Holy or the Divine, wear those. Remember: Accessories set us apart from the other animals!

Before you begin, decide your intention and purpose for creating a ritual for yourselves. Make agreements that you can not only fulfill but also embrace with open hearts.

The Session

A simple beginning would be to light a candle together while stating your collective intention. Enter your sacred space and begin by chanting *om* together for several minutes. Then move your focus to your breathing. Sit back to back and use the Golden Straw technique (see page 76). Then move so that one of you is lying back and receiving while the other is giving a pranic warm-up by passing his palms about one inch over the body, focusing on releasing golden energy. This is similar

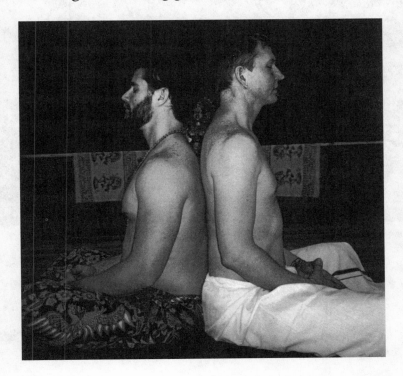

to painting your beloved with gold as transmitted through your hands. While receiving, continue with

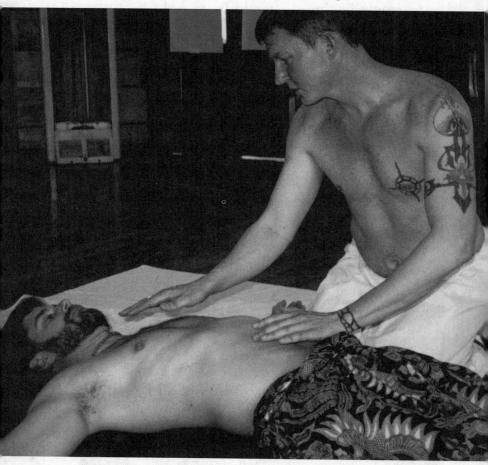

the Golden Straw breath technique, taking full and deep breaths. Gracefully come to trade roles. You are beginning to warm up and charge the body with prana as you cocreate your spiritual rocket fuel.

The experience will intensify if you take your

time with it and become detailed in your play. First, imagine painting gold the outer layer of skin, the epidermis. Can you direct the golden prana farther into him? Farther through all the skin layers to the muscles, tendons, and bone? To organs, blood, and cerebrospinal fluid? As you receive, how deeply can you accept this gift into your body? Returning to the conscious effort of your breathing will expand your experience. During the relaxation of your inhale, prana may seep more easily into you, blessing you and every cell of your body; enriching you, creating more life, oozing love.

This practice begins to wake up the esoteric anatomy that Tantra uses for advanced play. Some ways to help seal the open circuits of your body are to bring the soles of your feet together and bring your fingertips together: thumb to thumb, forefinger to forefinger, and so forth. Bringing the tongue to the position in the Golden Straw breathing meditation also helps open the brain centers. As you are receiving the pranic golden touch, you may feel moved to bring your arms over your head, with your fingertips touching while you bring your feet together at the soles.

Another practice to seal the container of your body is the root lock. By developing rapid anal

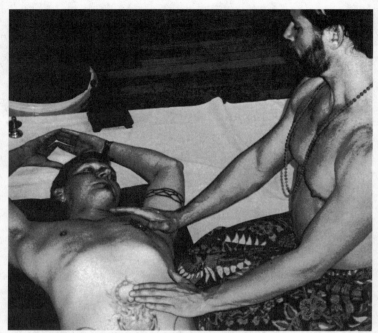

pumping of the perineum you create a peristalsis that stimulates the flow of cerebrospinal fluid (CSF) from the sacrum to the brain. This flow is very important in Tantra, as you bring your practice to the deep recesses of the brain cavities, where CSF and blood exchange.

Now transition to breathing on the skin, using a hot breath exhaled through an open throat and open mouth. Spending time exhaling onto the perineum can be especially delightful. Where you find a strong response as you breathe across your beloved, stay with him at that place and breathe with him to expand his feelings. Take turns fanning the golden sparks from your touch with the warm exhalations of your breath so that each of you feels adequately warmed up.

Next, move into your special way of honoring each other sexually and erotically. Is there a way to devote yourself and your efforts to his total pleasure? To focus solely on giving him what he asked for? Is there a way to follow your impulses and your hearts so that you take turns increasing each other's pleasure?

With the devotional aspect of Tantra, we honor our beloved as God. How is your approach different when you see him and worship him fully and unconditionally as a Divine Being? If you have a personal relationship with a Tantric, Egyptian, Buddhist, or Tibetan conception of God, or even with Jesus, can you deepen your focus and worship by addressing your beloved during your session as the embodiment of that aspect of the Divine—be it Hanuman, Skanda, Krishna, Ha-Shem, Isis, Jesus, or Tunkashila?

Frequently, it's difficult to receive and give touch at the same time. Sometimes while receiving you can intensify your experience by staying connected to your beloved through a gentle touch.

Sometimes depending on your style and practice, you might be holding on for dear life! Learning to receive is an important lesson. Many men rob themselves of great pleasure because they are always trying please their partners. The ebb and flow of life has both an active and a receptive pulse. Finding how to surf this erotic tide is also part of the process of creating and storing your spiritual rocket fuel.

TANTRIC SACRUM DRUMMING.

During the time of the Roman Empire, the men who named the bones in our bodies thought the soul resided in the sacrum. The word sacrum shares its root with English words such as sacred and sacristy. When we view the body from the perspective of Tantric esoteric anatomy, we realize the ancient Romans were not far off. While the "soul" doesn't have a single "home," the sacrum is the reservoir of Kundalini, the consciousness-expanding element we discussed earlier.

With practice, you can stimulate the rise of Kundalini. Here is one way for partners to help each other.

As your beloved lies on his stomach, sit comfortably at his side, perhaps on a cushion, and

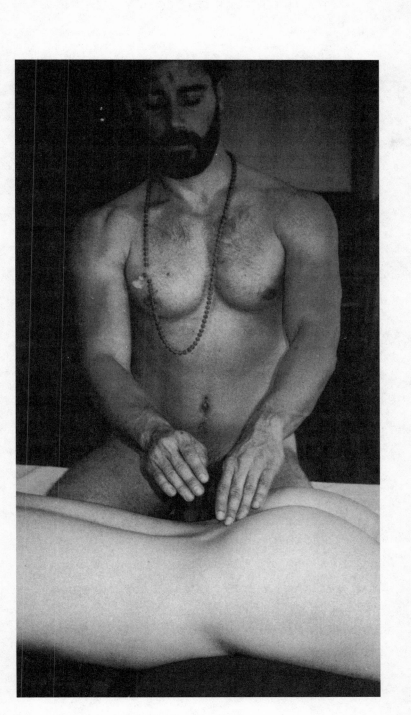

begin tapping his sacrum with your fingertips. Start gently and grow to more dynamic and physical contact. Move to hollow fists, always checking in with him about his comfort level with what you are doing. Be careful to stay on the triangular-shaped bone of the sacrum and avoid the tailbone or vertebrae. End by smoothing out the energy by making circles with an open palm in a clockwise position.

If you are receiving, keep the Golden Straw breath going as much as possible. The open-throat position is more of a feeling than an actual open throat since you are lying on your belly.

For more advanced play, instead of ending with open palm circles, end by rubbing the palm of your hand along his spine from sacrum to skull. Always travel up the spine, lifting your hand at the skull and then placing it on the sacrum to begin the stroke again. You can do this without oil and even use firm pressure to create friction. If the skin turns red, in most cases that's all right (unless it's accompanied by pain). When you receive this, time your breath so that you inhale as the stroke goes up your spine.

Connecting the Sacrum and the Base of the Skull
You can view the spine as a battery with two poles of opposite charge. One is at the sacrum, the

other at the top of the spine, where it enters the skull. More specifically, the top point of charge is the medulla oblongata. You can touch the surface of the sacrum through the skin, but you cannot directly palpate the medulla oblongata through the neck. But, though we cannot change the poles

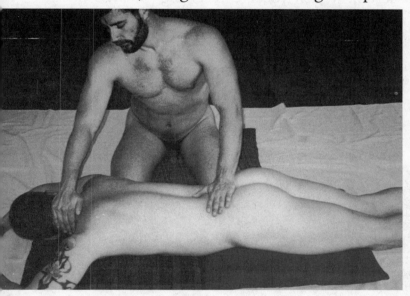

of a battery's charge, we can change the charge of the poles of the spine through touch, intention, and breath.

This practice best follows the Tantric sacrum drumming practice you just read about. Sit alongside your beloved so that one palm rests on his sacrum, the other on the back of his neck. Your hands should be very charged at this point. Begin breathing together with this visualization: On the exhale send golden energy from the palm over the sacrum so that it travels along the spine and ends at the skull, where you inhale. Repeat this at least seven times, always beginning the exhalation at the sacrum. When you are receiving, breathe in the opposite direction: As the receiver, inhale as your partner exhales. Set your intention to follow the flow of golden energy from the sacrum to the skull as you inhale. Exhale normally and begin again at the sacrum.

126

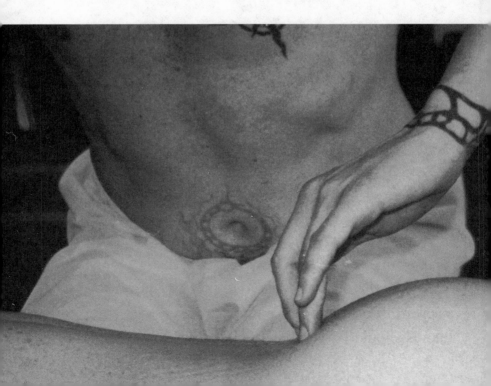

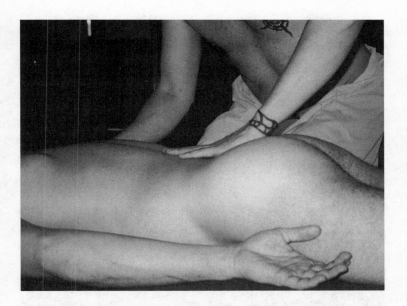

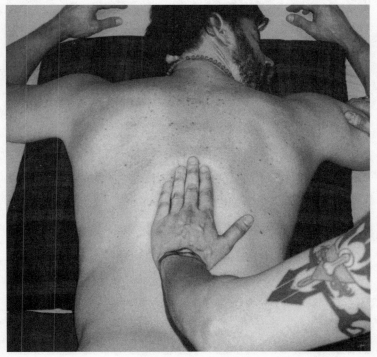

128

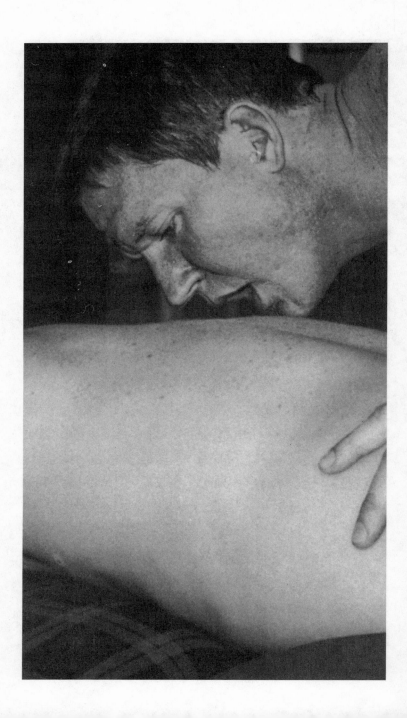

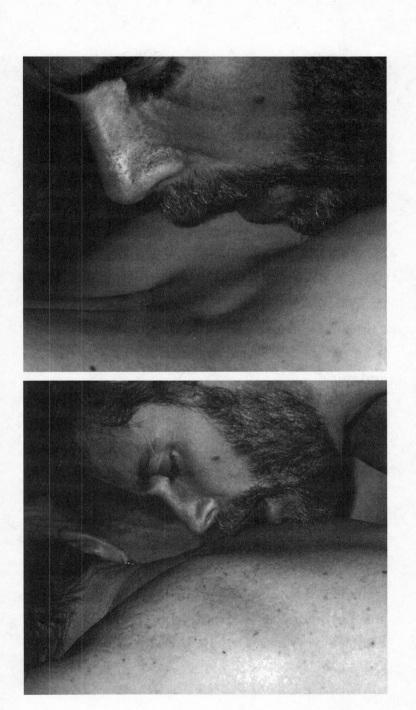

Sacred Cock Play

Now, with the pathways established, move into more direct sexual stimulation. While generating or receiving sexual touch to your genitals, continue the breathing patterns and golden visualizations. As you move to oral stimulation, maintain your breathing and focus on the pathways.

With practice you may experience the wonderful erect-cock feelings extending through your penis to your sacrum and then up your spine. Some men report feeling as though they have an erection that pierces their skull, brain, and mind.

External Perineum Stimulation

Now with your beloved lying on his back, take one palm and spread it wide across his perineum. Move it as you slowly continue to send golden energy into him, charging him with divine prana. The other hand may naturally find its way to his cock for more direct stimulation. As you receive, continue to breathe deeply. Stimulating his nipples and perineum at the same time can be another additive to your rocket fuel.

As you follow your erotic impulses and ride the edges of sensual delight, there are a few techniques that can help you extend these sensations or help you return to the moment.

Backward Ah

Use this technique as a way to surf the edges of orgasm. It's a terrific way to extend orgasm and help manage ejaculation. Just as in the Golden Straw technique, open your throat, inhaling as though you were saying "ah" during the inhale. This technique helps draw the sexual energy up the spine. For advanced play, you can inhale this way, but keep your tongue at the roof of your mouth. I feel that I pierce the brain centers more deeply when my tongue is pointing straight up into the center of the hard palate, like a hard cock. For really advanced play, allow your eyes to roll back, as though you were looking out the back of the crown of your head.

Breath

If you find your mind wandering, just return to the breath and to the experience. Returning to the experience of touch is a good way to reground yourself. If you find yourself remembering past experiences or traumas, just allow them to float away, knowing that whatever is important will be there for you at a more appropriate time. As emotions arise, feel welcome to express them as a way of releasing them. Always return to the breath, filling those lungs with the ebb and flow

132

full body orgasm:

Toward the end of a long night of much stimulation, my lover simply and lightly touched the back of my neck. His golden hands began at my neck very gently, massaging and relaxing the muscles. Slowly, I started to generate a lot of energy. I don't recall precisely what happened next. I remember fluttering around my ears, as if butterfly wings—many of them—were caressing my ears. His fingers of light carried the motion to the top of my head and swirled it up and above the apex. All of this happened in a minute or so; but the release I felt for literally several minutes had the intensity of a full body orgasm.

–Francisco M.

of oxygen, of prana, and of life. Sometimes making sounds can discharge negative thoughts or emotions.

Getting Unstuck

The best method for getting unstuck from a difficult place is to rotate your head back and forth. By doing this you shake the brain in its bath of cerebrospinal fluid, which usually kicks you into another space so that you can continue on your journey toward bliss.

Threshold

Each of us has different sexual and spiritual responses. It's important to know how your beloved responds, so that you can pick up on valuable cues. If he's riding a magic carpet through indescribable realms, you'll need to know how to best support him on his journey. It may be for you to slow down, distributing sexual touch throughout his body, or perhaps to allow him to simply let you witness his experience.

Orgasm

For our purposes, there are two types of orgasms: (1) internal orgasm without ejaculation and (2) external orgasm with ejaculation. In order to create, store, and then play with our sexual-spiritual rocket fuel, we have been managing the external orgasm to prolong our experience. At the beginning stages, there is a direct correlation between the time you and your beloved spend in a Tantric session and the intensity of your experience. One of the great advantages to taking more time is that you develop internal orgasms that come in waves through your body. One term for this is "edging," since it's like riding the edge of the wave as you surf on the sea of bliss. The Backward Ah will help you edge your way as you expand your session—remember, Tantra = "tools for expansion."

Some schools teach the avoidance of external orgasm that culminates in ejaculation. I agree that if your session is focused on your "getting off," you will probably miss any inherent spiritual opportunity.

Energetically, you have a great opportunity to truly blast through into new realms, riding the ejaculation as one of the deepest creative acts of man. I find this works best one partner at a time, because just as with the space shuttle, you blast off thundering with great speed. The experience then frequently becomes one of traveling through the realm of the gods.

With practice you can learn to time this experience together. But if you and your beloved are simultaneously preparing for blastoffs, it will be a challenge for each of you to release into your own experience.

RETURNING

All ritual has a beginning, middle, and end. I recommend you complete your session by returning to gazing into each other's eyes and then extinguishing the candle you lit earlier together. You will both be very impressionable and vulnerable at this time, so take great care with yourself and your partner. A simple heartfelt statement of gratitude will have a profound impact.

RECAPITULATION

This is the basic sequence for a Tantra session:

1. Practice the prana, breathing, and midsection exercises until you feel comfortable with them.
2. Set aside time when you will be rested and undisturbed.
3. Preset your space with everything you'll need for

the session. Remember to switch off the phone.

4. Prepare yourself, taking time and making the effort to create something special. Create your intention for the session.

5. Begin the session by lighting a candle or incense.

6. Chant *om* to center yourself and your partner.

7. Use this cycle during your session:
   - prana
   - breath
   - touch

8. Use the breath to actively stimulate prana and the rise of Kundalini through your spine. With your imagination see/feel/experience the erotic stimulation turn inward and upward, traveling through your head and brain centers.

9. When you are complete, acknowledge your session through gratitude. Extinguish the candle. As you return to reality, keep connected to the spiritual realms you entered during your session.

Conclusion

Change is constant. We can either react to it, or we can create our future with new actions taken daily. Tantra is for gay men who want to expand the spiritual dimensions in their lives. With Tantra we can cocreate a future of increasing divinity for ourselves through consciously creating new experiences. Tantra gives us a map so that we can create the best possible "now" for us—the best strategy for creating the most propitious future.

Tantra comes from time-tested practices that are as relevant in the 21st century as they were in ancient times. While Tantra is very personal, it is also very public as we grow to find divinity in all of life. Let's return to the parable of the flower. Can we extend this lesson from nature, in which we recognize that the flower needs air, water, soil, earth, compost, bugs, and bees to survive to the human realm? Can this flower be a metaphor for our daily interactions with others?

If you view this simple story as an explanation of creation and how creation is an act of the Divine Being, then you'll see that every element is divine.

Without any element, there would be no creation, and every element contributes to the process of creation. If creation is divine (and if human conception is one of the great examples of the ecstasy of creation) then all conspiring elements are also divine.

138

This may trouble some people who may ask, how can everything be divine? Does this story hold true when clearly there is a difference between good and evil in the world?

Is our spiritual perspective limited to a few very pretty but cut and wilting flowers? Or are we willing to embrace the messy dirt, the composting manure that makes the plant grow so robustly?

Is our spiritual life rarified like expensive nosegays, beautiful but dead? Or does it embrace all of the complex mycelia of a world as well as life clearly greater than our individual human imagination?

Is God just a Generator of things that makes us feel good—things we discard when they stop serving our immediate needs? Or can God also be the Operator of a complex weaving of life? Can God be the Dissolver of life?

How can the Generator, one of the roles of God, belong to the divine realm, but the others not?

To create, as we can conceive of it, are not the operating and dissolving functions needed as well?

So, is it all God? Is everything part of the process of the Divine?

Let's bring it closer to home.

If you're a registered, party-voting Democrat, can you also volunteer at the Log Cabin Club booth at your next Gay Pride event? At your next Pride parade, can you join the counterdemonstrators who preach death and destruction? Can we embrace Fred Phelps?

What may need to die? Is your world big enough to embrace all of these elements? I am reminded of my humanity as I recoil in horror at the repulsive thought of helping Fred Phelps. I don't need to support him, but can I see God in Mr. Phelps too? Can he inspire me to action that heals? If so, wouldn't that action be a function of God?

Conversely, think how many "spiritual" people today recoil in horror at the repulsive thought of helping gay men. Some play the mental game of loving the sinner but hating the sin.

In the Tantric cosmic view, there is only one unity. There is neither sinner nor sin. The illusion of separation from divine bliss is what keeps us stuck and provides suffering. Therefore, in Tantra we aim to find God and divinity and bliss in every moment. Can we do that even when we are in pain? Must humanity be the opposite of divinity? Can we circle back to the point of union from where we all began?

140

The divine unity of Tantra is at a deep level energetically inherent in our mind, body, and spirit. Everyone who has had an orgasm has glimpsed into this transcendence of the divisible world and into universes of bliss.

The spiritual technology of Tantra is available to everyone. It is inherent in the human body, and through practice, study, and initiation, you can expand your consciousness, using these tools to lead a full, rich, multifaceted life, going as far as you can go, using everything you are.

Namaste.

glossary

ACE: After the Common Epoch. Equivalent to A.D. (*anno Domini*), ACE is used to describe time for non-Christian cultures. While the Christian calendar has become the global calendar, ACE is used to honor cultures that don't describe themselves in Christian terms.

BCE: Before the Common Epoch. Equivalent to B.C. (before Christ). See explanation for usage of ACE.

Chela: Sanskrit for disciple, one who is pledged to a guru.

Ganesha: God with the body of a man and the head of an elephant.

Guru: Teacher. More specifically, a highly evolved teacher who is the embodiment of God to his followers.

Hanuman: God with the body of a man and the head of a monkey.

Kundalini: Sanskrit for a coiled serpent that is anthropomorphized as a female power. The coiled serpent rests at the base of the spine. When awakened to rise, like a cobra it expands consciousness. Kundalini arousal is a goal of many yogic practices.

Lingam: Sanskrit for penis.

Mantra: Sanskrit for "tools for the mind," i.e., sounds or chants that have been handed down from antiquity. These align the practitioner with specific divine qualities.

Om: Sanskrit word that represents the seed sound of creation.

Prana: Sanskrit for life force, an esoteric substance that is the basis of existence (like *chi* in traditional Chinese medicine).

Pranayama: Exercises that include breathing and often visualization.

Rajas: Sanskrit for the principle of motion.

Sattva: Sanskrit for the principle of goodness, virtue, productive knowledge, and tranquility.

Shaivism: Branch of Hinduism that venerates the god Shiva. The term is sometimes rendered as Shivaism or Sivaism.

Shakti: Shiva's consort as well as the feminine principle, which is considered the power that creates forward motion.

Shiva: One of the three male attributes of God. Shiva is considered the god of time, dance, and dissolution.

Siddhi: Sanskrit for "accomplishment," specifically one of eight accomplishments that many spiritual seekers obtain during their lifetime.

Skanda: Son of Shiva, born out of the union of Shiva's semen with fire. The name literally means "jet of sperm." God of perpetual youth, Skanda leads armies and is opposed to marriage.

Swami: Sanskrit for "one's own master." A swami may be part of a religious order and is thus similar to a monk in Christianity.

Tamas: Sanskrit for the principle of dullness or density.

Tantra: Sanskrit word meaning "tools for expansion." The Tantras refer to the body of written materials that contains the rites and rituals of the Shaivism religion.

Yantra: Sanskrit for "conception tool." The geometric representation of mantra.

Yoga: Sanskrit for union with the Divine.

Yoni: Sanskrit for vagina.

144

RESOURCES

Tantra—Basic

Mumford, Jonn (Swami Anandakapila Saraswati). *A Chakra & Kundalini Workbook: Psycho-Spiritual Techniques for Health, Rejuvenation, Psychic Powers, and Spiritual Realization.* 4th ed. Llewellyn Publications (www.llewellyn.com), 1994.

Along with *Ecstasy Through Tantra,* this book is a must-have for all students of Tantra. Swami Anandakapila, a.k.a. Dr. Jonn Mumford, outlines very detailed practices in this book. With his training as a chiropractor and a psychotherapist as well as his initiation into Hindu orders (Saraswati and Giri), he has a unique vantage point that is extremely helpful for Western students. This book includes a 12-week practice plan so that you may incorporate—put into your own body—this very valuable information.

Mumford, Jonn, and Carl Llewellyn Weschke (Introduction). *Ecstasy Through Tantra*. Llewellyn Publications, 1988.

This is the best book about Tantra for the Western reader, and it makes very clear the spiritual dimensions inherent in sexual expression. Dr. Mumford uncovers and explores the esoteric anatomy that forms the basis of Tantric sexual ritual and then reveals how to incorporate it into your spiritual practice. This book is directed at heterosexuals, but in most cases the information is applicable to gay men.

Sunyata Saraswati and Bodhi Avinasha. *Jewel in the Lotus, The Tantric Path to Higher Consciousness*. Sunstar Publishing Ltd., 1995.

Sunyata Saraswati is one of America's most influential Tantra teachers. He has taught, coached, and given initiation to many of the leaders of the heterosexual Tantra community in the United States. This book is a systemic course on Tantric Kriya Yoga. Although written for heterosexuals, much of the information and many of the exercises can be useful to gay men. Bodhi Avinasha is the leader of Ipsalu Tantra. I hold a teaching credential in Ipsalu Tantra from her organization.

Tantra—Advanced

Avalon, Arthur (Sir John Woodroffe). *Introduction to Tantra Sastra*. Auromere Books, 1980, reprint.

Sir John Woodroffe (1865-1936) was a British judge in Calcutta who had his first encounter with Tantra quite by accident. Afterward, he decided to undergo initiation into Hindu ritual and subsequently became the first translator of Tantra texts into English. He published his translations and writings on Tantra under the name Arthur Avalon. Though very technical and densely written, this set of essays is a wellspring of information for the serious student of Tantra.

Avalon, Arthur (Introduction). Trans. and ed. M.P. Pandit and Taranatha Vidyaratna. *Kularnava Tantra*. Motilal Banarsidass Publishers, 2000, reprint.

Woodroffe's English introduction dates from the first Western publication of this Sanskrit text in 1916. Following his introduction is an English rendering of the texts by scholar M.P. Pandit. For purists, the original Sanskrit text makes up the remainder of the book. This text forms what we know to be the basis of Kaula Tantra, which flourished in the 13th century BCE. In the preface, Pandit writes:

148

> The principle of Tantra is to reject nothing that God has created, to utilize every means to raise the human consciousness to the Divine. Unlike many of the older systems, Tantra is highly rational in its approach; it asks for no faith in advance. It is a self-verifying science of the development of natural energies into the supernatural terms leading to a cosmic enjoyment of life in a spiritual consciousness.

Swami Satyananda Saraswati. *Kundalini Tantra*. Bihar School of Yoga, 1996.

Written by the former head of the Saraswati order, this advanced book clearly describes the phenomenon of Kundalini. *Ecstasy through Tantra* is dedicated to this author, who initiated Swami Anandakapila into the Saraswati order in the

1970s. The fourth section of this volume is by a different author whose writing is not as cogent, intelligent, and engaging as that of Satyananda's first three sections. Still, this is one of the most dog-eared books on my nightstand.

Queer Hindu

Pattanaik, Devdutt, ed. *The Man Who Was a Woman and Other Queer Tales From Hindu Lore.* Harrington Park Press, 2001.

Dr. Pattanaik has compiled 71 stories taken from the broad pantheon of Hindu mythology of gods and goddesses who trade genders, cross-dress, or become castrated. Each story is prefaced with a brief but informative commentary to deepen the reader's understanding.

Vanita, Ruth, ed. *Queering India: Same-Sex love and Eroticism in Indian Culture and Society.* Routledge, 2001.

This book was written with academic rigor and precision and therefore may be too dry and technical for some readers. Full of facts and history, it helps the reader understand the cultural shifts and historical events that have made gay life in India what is today.

Vanita, Ruth, and Saleem Kidwai, eds. *Same-Sex Love in India*. St. Martin's, 2001.

This book is a selection of primary sources on same-sex love, both ancient as well as modern texts, all of which have been translated into English. Each text is prefaced with an introduction designed to help the reader understand the writing's context. The ancient and medieval sections are very scholarly. The modern section speaks for itself.

150

Hinduism

Daniélou, Alain, ed. and trans. *The Complete Kama Sutra*. Inner Traditions International Ltd., 1994.

This is the best available translation of the *Kama Sutra*. Alain Daniélou was the first openly gay Westerner to be initiated into Hindu rituals who later wrote about his experiences. Daniélou's translations and detailed explications of the texts skillfully paint a fascinating portrait of the medieval India that gave birth to this famous text.

Daniélou, Alain. *Gods of Love and Ecstasy: The Traditions*

of Shiva and Dionysus. Inner Traditions International Ltd., 1992.

Here Daniélou explores the parallels between the Greek God Dionysus and the Hindu God Shiva and traces them through modern times. As a gay man, Daniélou shares with us some compelling translations:

> The phallus is the source of pleasure. It is
> the only means of obtaining earthly
> pleasure and salvation. By looking at it,
> touching it and meditating on it, living
> beings can free themselves from the cycle
> of future lives.
> *Shiva Purana, Vidyeshvara-Samhita I,*
> Chapter 9, verse 20.

Daniélou, Alain. *The Way to the Labyrinth: Memories of East and West.* New Directions, 1987.

This is Daniélou's autobiography. Outspoken and out as a gay man, Daniélou describes in detail much about his amazing journey between East and West. Even though he was born to an upper-class French background in the early 20th century, his life reads like a 19th-century adventure. Through his own might and determination, he became one of the 20th century's leading Indologists and ethnomusicologists. Daniélou is remarkably open about his life, including its gay male aspects. An interesting fact is that it was through his boyhood friendship with the current king of Afghanistan, Zahir Shah, he was introduced to the traditions of the Orient and India.

Daniélou, Alain. *While the Gods Play: Shaiva Oracles and Predictions on the Cycles of History and the Destiny of Mankind*. Inner Traditions International Ltd., 1987.

Fluent in both Sanskrit and Tamil, Daniélou writes and translates engagingly and with great authority. This is one of my most underlined books. In the section "Social Man," Daniélou writes:

> Since they are not involved in reproduction, and since this breaks the genetic chain, homosexuals fall outside the castes. One of their functions is to establish links between the different castes and races and also between men, spirits and the gods. They play a key part in magical practices.

Yoga

Feuerstein, Georg. *The Yoga Tradition: Its History, Literature, Philosophy and Practice*. Hohm Press, 2001.

If you buy just one book on yoga, this is the one. Very detailed and engaging and in a large format with photographs and drawings, this will become your touchstone and ultimate reference book for yoga. In addition, each chapter includes source readings that give readers a well-rounded picture. In the final section, titled "Power and Transcendence in Tantrism," Feuerstein says, "Mastery of basic yogic techniques is helpful since they form the building blocks of the transcendent ritual and worship that is Tantra—liberation through expansion."

Classes

I periodically offer classes in Tantra for gay men. For details, visit my Web site (listed below) at www.gaytantra.com.

The Body Electric School
6527A Telegraph Avenue
Oakland, CA 94609
(510) 653-1594
www.bodyelectric.org

Based in Oakland, Calif., the Body Electric School offers many classes on massage, sexuality, sacred sex, and sexual healing. They also offer classes in yoga and Tantra for gay men. Most of their classes are held throughout the United States. Advanced work is often conducted at their Wildwood Retreat Center in Northern California.

154

Web Sites

Ashram of Swami Pranavananda Brahmendra Avadutha Swamigal
www.aumnamahshivaya.org

Swami Pranavananda Brahmendra Avadutha Swamigal maintains an ashram dedicated to Shiva in the Kolli Hills of South India. He is one of only two "out" gay swamis whom I know of. Through the Internet he is available for consultations as well as dialogue. He writes: "I welcome true seekers who want to join us in our pursuit of merging with Lord Shiva and devoting one's life to Him."

The Feldenkrais Guild of North America (FGNA)
www.feldenkrais.com

This Web site offers several online courses in Awareness Through Movement (ATM), through which you can sample the Feldenkrais method of somatic education.

GayTantra.com
www.gaytantra.com
This is my Web site, where you'll find information about classes, recordings, and future publications. You can also use it to meet men interested in Tantra in your area.

Gay Tantra: Sacred Sexuality, Bodywork, and Massage
www.gaytantra.net
This colorful site was created by Toronto-based erotic masseur Serge Grandbois and offers a wealth of information that is relevant to Tantra and gay men.

The Official Dr. Jonn Mumford Consultation Site
www.jonnmumfordconsult.com
Through the beauty, speed, and the relative immediacy of the Internet, you too may study with Swami Anandakapila. His course is well-suited for gay men and incorporates concepts and techniques from his two books, *Ecstasy Through Tantra* and *A Chakra & Kundalini Workbook*.

The Rolf Institute of Structural Integration
www.rolf.org

This comprehensive Web site for the Rolf Institute based in Boulder, Colo., provides a good introduction to structural integration and lists Rolf practitioners throughout the country.

Tantra
www.tantrapm.com

This Web site offers great information from two of Swami Anandakapila's senior students who are also very good friends of mine and have opened their hearts to assist me. Both Umeshanand and Veenanand are as solid as diamond in their resolve to educate and teach Tantra as it was originally intended to be practiced.